Seaside
Quilts

Quilting & Sewing Projects for Beach-Inspired Décor

Seaside Quilts

Quilting & Sewing Projects for Beach-Inspired Décor

Carol C. Porter & Rebecca J. Hansen

Design Originals

an Imprint of Fox Chapel Publishing
www.d-originals.com

Acquisition editor: Peg Couch

Copy editor: Ayleen Stellhorn

Cover and layout designer: Ashley Millhouse

Photography: Peg Couch, Rebecca J. Hansen,
J. Horn, Scott Kriner, G. Liley, Ashley Millhouse,
Carol C. Porter, Lexi Weeber

Editor: Katie Weeber

ISBN 978-1-57421-431-4

Library of Congress Cataloging-in-Publication Data

Porter, Carol C., 1948-
  Seaside quilts / Carol C. Porter, Rebecca J Hansen.
    page cm
  Includes index.
  Summary: " Quilting Projects Beach & Cottage Style shows how to transform any dwelling into a relaxing shore retreat, with sea-inspired linens and home decor. This book presents dozens of simple, beautiful projects, with inspirational ideas for sewing, painting and crafting a love affair with the ocean. Readers will discover charming ways to enhance bedrooms, bathrooms, kitchens or family spaces with coordinating seaside hues and matching coastal themes. Anyone with a little craft or quilting knowledge can make these accessible and engaging projects, which range from quilts, wall hangings and cushions to tablecloths, pot holders and tea towels. With gorgeous color photographs and easy-to-follow instructions, this book will enable readers to stylishly decorate an entire seaside home, or just give an ordinary room anywhere a lovely seaboard motif"-- Provided by publisher.
  ISBN 978-1-57421-431-4 (pbk.)
  1. Patchwork--Patterns. 2. Quilting--Patterns. I. Hansen, Rebecca J. II. Title.
  TT835.P6455 2014
  746.46--dc23
              2013017337

©2014 by Carol C. Porter, Rebecca J. Hansen, and New Design Originals Corporation, www.d-originals.com, an imprint of Fox Chapel Publishing, 800-457-9112, 1970 Broad Street, East Petersburg, PA 17520.

Printed in China
First printing

About the Authors

Carol C. Porter

Carol is the Education Director for Clover Needlecraft Incorporated, where she helps make the company's many unique products accessible and engaging. She is an accomplished author, designer, sewer, quilter, knitter, pattern maker, and crafter. Carol is also a disciplined and thoughtful teacher whose encouragement and patience regularly inspires student creativity and success. Carol is recognized for the strength of her "colorwash" designs and has produced quilt patterns under the Heatherworks label. Carol is coauthor of *Patchwork Pantry*, *Pretty and Pieced*, and has designs in *Quilted for Christmas*. Recently she has authored *Making Jewelry with a French Knitter* and coauthored *Bead Weaving on a Loom*.

Rebecca J. Hansen

A well-respected quilting teacher, Beckie has been sewing since the age of 12 and took her first quilting class in the fall of 1989. Her quilt designs have appeared in popular quilt books, including *Angle Antics*, *Woven Ribbons*, *Cubic Ribbons*, *Strips That Sizzle*, *Easy Reversible Vests*, *Patchwork Pantry*, *Patchwork Picnic*, *Machine Quilting Made Easy*, and *Machine Quilting with Decorative Threads*. Beckie's quilts are also in collections including Marilyn Doheny and the Grays Harbor Community Hospital. As a quilting teacher, Beckie does programs for local quilt guilds and takes on community projects such as making baby quilts for the University of Washington Medical Center and providing quilts for raffles, auctions, and fundraising. Besides quilting, Beckie enjoys decorative painting, faux painting treatments, window glass etching, and refreshing old furniture.

Table of Contents

Techniques .122

Appliqué and Embroidery Patterns. 131

Acknowledgments 140

Index. 142

26

62

76

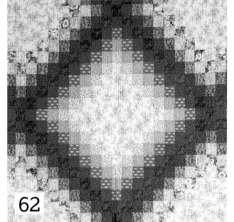

36

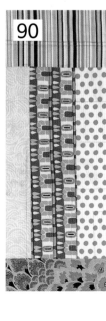

90

94

54

Introduction

If you've picked up this book, we know you love the beach. Perhaps you are drawn to the vast array of colors that can be found along the shoreline, or the wildlife you've encountered and the items you've collected. Or perhaps you are drawn by wonderful memories of friends and family and the activities you shared together. *Seaside Quilts* is an adventure through the art of quilt making and bringing what you love about the ocean to light in your quilt designs.

Every project springs directly from seaside inspirations, which are featured at the beginning of each project. Discover how to use favorite wildlife or shell shapes to create appliqué or quilting designs. Learn to build a color palette based on the subtle pastels of beach glass, blue and white ocean waves, or tan and brown sandy shores. Transform a favorite beach scene into a quilt top. Written instructions and illustrations will guide you along the way as you turn your inspiration and ideas into pieces that perfectly capture your love for the beach.

Along the way, you will find wonderful tips for showcasing beach collections, creating beach-themed home décor pieces, and infusing rooms with seaside style.

This book is geared to empower creativity and stimulate ideas. Take what you learn about going from inspiration to design to create your very own seaside quilts and projects. We love using our quilts and designs to reflect our style and personality, and we encourage you to do the same.

We invite you to join us as we share our combined creativity, excitement, awe, peace, and discovery that come from *Seaside Quilts*.

Carol C. Porter and Rebecca J. Hansen

Be willing to be surprised by what might suggest a color palette, such as beach-inspired fabric, postcards, photographs, artwork, and glassware.

Flora and Fauna

Shore Birds

Tidal Pool

Glassware

Notice the color palette associated with beach activities like sunbathing, boating, surfing, kite flying, reading, playing in the sand, and celebrating with a bonfire.

Umbrellas

Beach Bags

Beach Towels

Beach Balls

Surfboards

Bonfire

Boats

A trip to the paint store will yield paint chips with names like Ocean Breeze, Surf's Up, Seaport, Tranquil Sea, Caribbean Green, Coastal Mist, Sunrise Beach, Coral Dune, Malibu Peach, and on and on. Throughout the book we will make reference to those things that were influential in our design and color choices.

For purposes of design and construction, we were attracted to
quilt blocks that have seaworthy names:

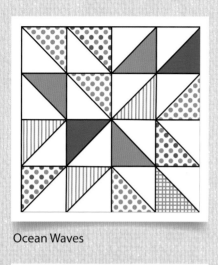

Ocean Waves

Storm at Sea

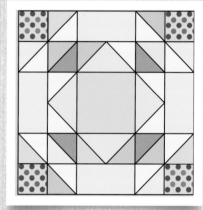

Summer Winds

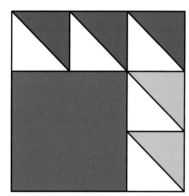

Birds in the Air

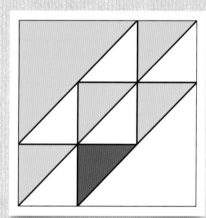

Nautilus

Northwind

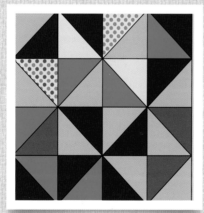

Port & Starboard

Flying Geese

Seaside Inspiration
for Quilters

The projects throughout this book are infused with coastal colors and contain appliqué and quilting motifs inspired by beach and ocean wildlife. Beckie built the design of her beach home around these same inspirations, creating a look that perfectly complements her sea-inspired quilts. Let Beckie's use of color and beach collections in her home décor spark your creativity to build a design around your own seaside quilt.

The master bedroom.
The Seaside Serenade quilt makes a gorgeous centerpiece for the master bedroom. Complementary green and peach colors were used to paint the walls, creating a refreshing palette that brings to mind foamy ocean waves and seashells.

G. LILEY

G. LILEY

The master bath. The adjoining bath carries over the green and peach paint colors from the master bedroom. Antique light fixtures with peach shades continue the color scheme. The windows surrounding the bathtub are etched with an underwater fish scene to obscure the view inside. A wonderful surprise is the reflection of the fish and grasses when light comes through the window and the scene is transferred onto the cabinets and blinds.

The great room. The deep sea blue accent wall in the great room makes the perfect backdrop on which to showcase the Seaside Bounty wall hanging. The quilt's bright appliqué and border design make it pop against the darker blue and are the perfect reminder of what's just outside—even in the winter. The room is also home to several beach collections. Sand pails are placed on the curved sand-colored ledge overlooking the room, while a vintage typesetter's tray, filled with shells collected by grandchildren and fitted with a glass top, spans two ottomans. An expansive fireplace provides welcome memories for family and friends gathered around the room on cool summer evenings. The stone face of the fireplace is reminiscent of the color of driftwood, while the bold and beautifully crafted mantle and fireplace casing bring to mind a well-varnished seaworthy sailboat.

The dining room. A relaxing blue/green color brings the feel of the ocean and sky into the dining room and encourages guests and family to linger in conversation or just relax to the sound of the ocean waves. Along the top of the walls, a stencil was used to apply joint compound highlighted with iridescent paint to create a subtle decorative border. Quilted seasonal table runners and placemats are a perfect addition to a seasonal celebration. Beckie likes to make reversible pieces that can perform double duty throughout the year.

The stairwell. The stairwell and landings are used to show off various family and beach collections. Three oars are used in place of traditional banisters. Beach glass lines the window shelf, while the first landing features antiques and vintage family photos of a first summer at the beach. The upper landing features a wave design on the wall, with a cheerful yellow color that continues into the guest bedroom. This bright area is an ideal spot to show off some favorite things, including some small quilted pieces.

G. LILEY

G. LILEY

The guest bedroom. The guest bedroom is filled with windows that flood the room with natural light. The light is accentuated by the soft yellow paint, creating the feeling of sitting on the beach under the sun. Guests feel right at home in a room that contains treasured family antique furniture, memorabilia, and linens. The bed skirt is made to be reversible so different bedspreads, including basket motif summer throws, chenille spreads, and the Beach Glass quilt can be used on the bed depending on the season. Smaller collected quilts and linens are at home on the foot of the bed or the nearby chairs.

The breakfast room. Filled with light, the breakfast room invites you to sit and enjoy the morning sun. The pillows and bench seat cushions are reversible, providing the option for different looks throughout the year. Oversize quilted potholders can be seen on the pillow fronts, creating a unique look that is easily customized. This casual setting invites the use of fun and colorful quilted table runners and placemats, like the Beach Glass placemats pictured.

J. HORN

The sunroom. Just down the hall from the sewing space, the sunroom draws you in with its abundance of light and sea green walls. It makes a perfect place for an afternoon of stitching a seaside quilt or creating home décor projects with friends. The room is decorated with a daybed filled with quilt-block pillows and vintage linens, vintage folding chairs with collected linens, and a cushy bench. Smaller quilts sit atop creamy yellow cabinets and fill the shelves below. The doorknobs are fashioned from thread spools, which are also used throughout the room in other aspects of the décor.

G. LILEY

G. LILEY

G. LILEY

The sewing space. The sewing space is out in the open, overlooking the great room. It has an unobstructed view of the ocean, providing incredible inspiration for seaside quilt projects. Even the countertop brings the feel of the beach into the space, pieced together to make the area near the railing look like deep ocean water and the cutting area like the sandy beach.

The kids' room. The Ocean Waves: Under the Sea quilt establishes an ocean theme in the kids' room, which is complemented by bright fish-shaped pillows. The high plate rail makes the perfect place to display beach finds, pictures, and theme pieces. Just under the shelf, vintage knobs provide a place for small quilts and other treasures to be displayed.

Using Beach and
Other Collections

Beaches bring out the collector in most of us—and Beckie and I are no exception. Every time I go to a beach, I return home with a trove of shells, beach glass, rocks, and driftwood. I used to put my collection in a shoebox in the garage with every intention of crafting something wonderful out of it in the future. What was once treasure found quickly became treasure stashed! One of my lessons from working on this book is that there are many ways in which to showcase such special pieces. Now, these ever-present finds bring back memories of warm sand and family time.

Beckie collects beach glass and shells, antique kitchenware, and special glassware. Her husband collects sand pails. They both collect so much more, but they fold their finds into their beach home in beautiful and clever ways. Beckie also started collecting linens more than twenty years ago. Her intent was to collect quilts with basket themes. Having no luck finding them, she realized that there were plenty of linens with the basket motif, and so her collection was born. The variety is endless: dresser scarves, table toppers, summer throws, chenille bedspreads, and arm chair covers to name a few. These linens are always put to good use and are pleasing to discover.

Other artful ways of using beach finds such as shells, rocks, and beach glass include ornaments, vase fillers surrounding a candle, a place card holder, or just about anything you can imagine. Many projects can include the entire family...rocks and shells for a game of checkers or tic-tac-toe. Collections of found objects or inherited treasures yearn to be seen and showcased. What do you gather, and how will you share it with all to see?

Shells find a home in an old muffin tin.

G. LILEY

Milk Glass displayed in an open corner of the dining room.

Layers of quilts piled to capacity stay protected in a wooden hutch.

Found beach glass or shells make great filler for a plant pot.

These old suitcases are stacked on a low refurbished and painted table topped with a "caged" green plant. A place of honor for past memories, this is a great visual and textural spot for any home decoration.

Suitcases are an ideal storage container for just some of Beckie's linen collection.

Quilt Projects

Sea-inspired quilt projects are a perfect way to set the scene for a beach-themed room or to adorn a beach house. Large projects like the Beach Glass Quilt or the Seaside Serenade Quilt make excellent centerpieces for a room's décor, while smaller projects like the Sand Treasures or Seaside Bounty Wall Hangings can add the perfect seaside touch to an entryway or bathroom. Be sure to integrate colors and themes that you see around you in these projects, and they're sure to be a perfect fit. Or, use them to add to the colors and themes your home currently has.

Beach Glass Quilt

DIMENSIONS: 58¼" x 70½" (122.5 x 179cm)

With boundless spirit, ocean waves and surging tides carry beach glass and shell shards to every shore. Polished to a satin finish, they arrive as clear glass, in shades of green and brown, and even blue or violet. And sometimes, you can find a rare red or rose. This quilt celebrates the beautiful array of beach glass and shell colors.

Fabric Requirements

- ☐ 1½ yd. (150cm) white for center squares and Flying Geese backgrounds
- ☐ 2½ yd. (250cm) ecru and white print for backgrounds and border
- ☐ 20 assorted fat quarters (45.5 x 56cm) in beach glass and shell colors
- ☐ ½ yd. (50cm) each, 2 Asian prints
- ☐ ½ yd. (50cm) binding
- ☐ Backing and batting

J. HORN

About Metric

Throughout this book, you'll notice that every measurement is accompanied by a metric equivalent. Inches and yards are rounded off to the nearest half or whole centimeter unless precision is necessary. Please be aware that while this book will show 1 yard = 100 centimeters, the actual conversion is 1 yard = 90 centimeters, a difference of about 3¹⁵⁄₁₆" (10cm). Using these conversions, you will always have a little bit of extra fabric if purchasing by the metric quantity.

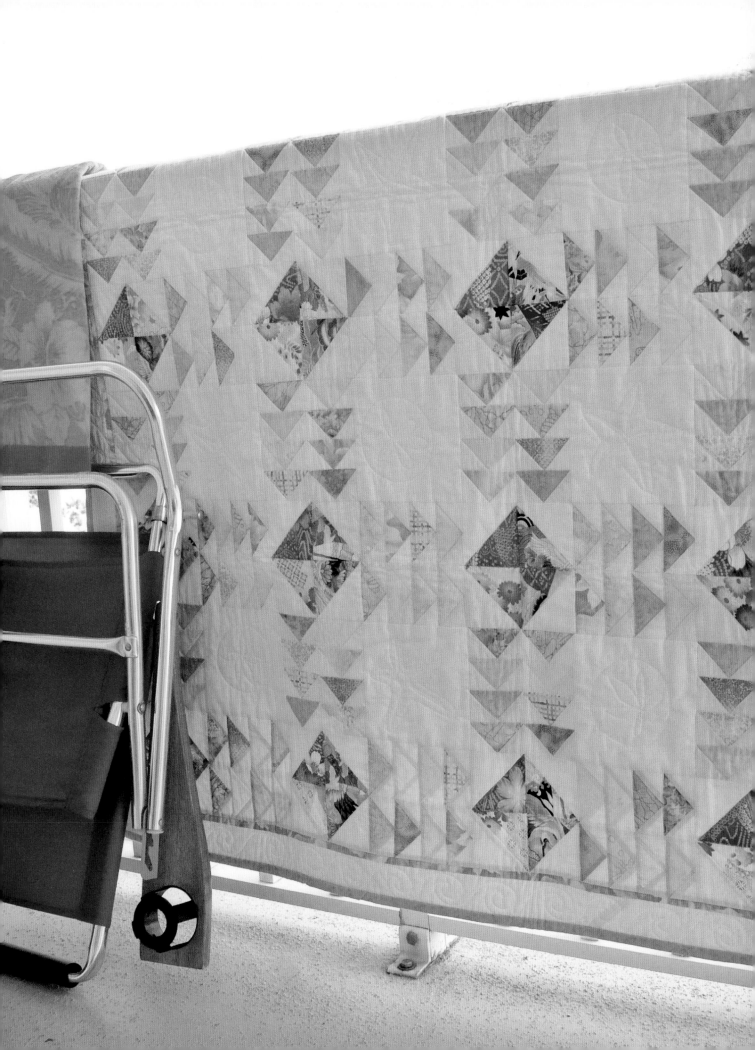

Cutting & Sewing Directions

FLYING GEESE UNITS

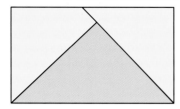

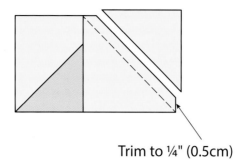

Trim to ¼" (0.5cm)

4. Repeat with the second square on the right side of the rectangle.

1. To make the Flying Geese units, cut 1 rectangle 2" x 3½" (5 x 9cm).

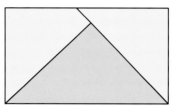

Trim to 2" x 3½" (5 x 9cm)

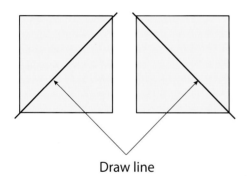

Draw line

2. Cut 2 squares each 2" x 2" (5 x 5cm). Draw a diagonal line on each square from corner to corner.

Trim to ¼" (0.5cm)

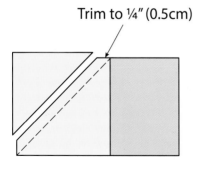

3. Place 1 square on the left side of the rectangle with right sides together; sew on the diagonal line. Trim the seam to ¼" (0.5cm) and press the triangle up.

5. The Flying Geese unit should measure 2" x 3½" (5 x 9cm). The quilt requires 392 units. Note: There is some waste with this method; however, many quilters agree that working with squares is easier and faster than working with small triangles. It takes 16 units for 1 square. Although the required total of 392 units may seem daunting, making 16 at a time is quite doable. Pace yourself and make it fun!

HALF-SQUARE TRIANGLE UNITS

Note: There are several methods to cut Half-Square Triangle units. The method we are using here works well when using scraps. For illustrations, see Step 3 on page 45.

1. Cut 1 square 3⅞" (10cm) from the ecru or white, and cut 1 square 3⅞" (10cm) from an Asian print.

2. Layer these squares right sides together and draw a line diagonally from corner to corner.

3. Stitch ¼" (0.5cm) from both sides of the diagonal line.

4. Cut on the diagonal line. Open, press seam to the dark, and trim to 3½" x 3½" (9 x 9cm). This will yield 2 Half-Square Triangle units. Make 60 pairs using this method for a yield of 120 units.

BEACH GLASS BLOCK

1. For the center square, cut a 6½" x 6½" (16.5 x 16.5cm) square from the white fabric. Cut 20 squares.

2. Piece together as shown. You'll need 16 Flying Geese units and 4 Half-Square Triangle units for each block.

QUILT TOP ASSEMBLY

1. To assemble the quilt top, make 20 Beach Glass blocks. Trim each to 12½" (32cm).

2. Lay out 4 blocks across and 5 blocks down, and sew them together in rows, making sure to press the seams in opposite directions from row to row. Press joining row seams all in one direction.

Beach Glass Block
Make 20

PIECED BORDER

The pieced border is made from 18 pieced units and 4 corner Half-Square Triangle units. Sew together as pictured.

ACCENT & OUTER BORDERS

The accent border is cut 1" (2.5cm) wide with enough strips to equal each side and top and bottom border. Fold the accent border in half with wrong sides together and baste. Or, place it on top of the right side of the outer border and sew it in place as you sew the outer border to the quilt top.

For the outer border, cut 8 strips, each 3" (7.5cm) wide by the width of the fabric from selvage to selvage. Measure the sides of the quilt, and sew enough strips to equal this length plus 8" (20.5cm) for mitered corners. Join the strips end to end. Measure the top and bottom of the quilt top, and add 8" (20.5cm) to those measurements for mitering. See Mitered Corners on page 126 for more information.

FINISHING

1. Mark the quilt top using a design of your choice.

2. Layer the quilt top with the batting and backing; baste it in place.

3. Quilt as desired, and then bind the edges.

4. Add a label, and sign, date, and photograph your finished quilt.

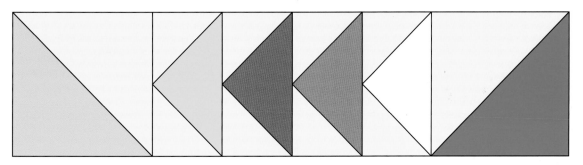

Pieced Border
Make 18

Beach Glass Wall Hanging

DIMENSIONS: 30" x 30" (76 x 76cm)

Birds gotta sing; geese gotta fly. Hang this on the wall or use it as a table topper. In either case, this is a great backdrop to showcase your beach glass and shell collection.

Project Directions

The construction for this piece is the same as that used for the Beach Glass Quilt (see page 26). Notice that here the Flying Geese units are "flying" in different directions, which makes the quilt hanging seem busier than the quilt. There are no rules when it comes to the Flying Geese units; place them in a way that appeals to you.

This piece is very manageable and a good one for machine quilting practice. Mark the quilting design (we put shorebirds in the squares), layer the batting and backing, and have fun quilting. Remember to sign and date your work when you are finished.

Materials

- ☐ ¼ yd. (25cm) white
- ☐ ½ yd. (50cm) ecru/ white print
- ☐ 20 assorted fat quarters (45.5 x 56cm) or scraps from quilt project in beach glass and shell colors
- ☐ ¼ yd. (25cm) each, 2 Asian prints
- ☐ Backing, binding, and batting

G. LILEY

While shells and beach glass inspired the color palette for this design, the abundant shore birds inspired the quilting in the white center squares.

Quilt Top Assembly

Make 4 Beach Glass blocks, 4 corner Half-Square Triangle
units, and 8 Pieced Border units.

Beach Glass Placemat Set

DIMENSIONS: 12½" x 18½" (32 x 47cm)

Shrimp cocktails, clam chowder, fresh fruit, coffee or tea, and a slice of crusty bread presented on these placemats will have your guests celebrating your culinary skills and their good fortune. Materials and sewing directions are the same as for the Beach Glass Wall Hanging.

J. HORN

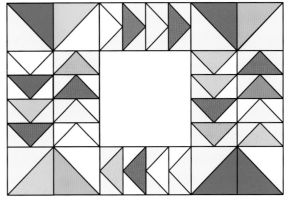

Placemat Assembly

Make 1 Beach Glass block and 2 Pieced Border units.

Sand Treasures Quilt

DIMENSIONS: 57" x 57" (145 x 145cm)

Twice a day ocean tides serve up wondrous treasures from the sea. Some are nature's bounty; others mark the hand of man. While we earnestly gather collections of these treasures with visions of future craft and décor projects, many slip into obscurity in unattended buckets and bags. This quilt allows you to display these items all the time. Sand Treasures is done in muted sandy colors with raw-edge appliqué at the center of the blocks. The motifs are some of those special items that might be found washed ashore.

Fabric Requirements

- ☐ 20–24 assorted fat quarters (45.5 x 56cm) in off-white, ecru, and tans for top and borders
- ☐ ¾ yd. (75cm) tan for side and corner triangles
- ☐ Assorted colors and textures for appliqué
- ☐ ½ yd. (50cm) tan for binding
- ☐ Batting and backing

A collection of beach treasures like those shown here inspired the design for this quilt.

Tip

Always check your scraps before shopping for fabric. You might have a stash of the necessary colors on hand already.

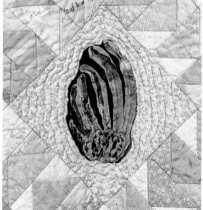

Cutting & Sewing Directions

1. Make 13 Beach Glass blocks following the directions for the Beach Glass Quilt (see page 26), but cut each center square for the blocks 1" (25mm) larger (7½" x 7½" [19 x 19cm]). This will accommodate shrinkage that may occur from sewing on the appliqué. Work the appliqué before sewing the blocks. See Raw-Edge Appliqué on page 130 for more information.

2. Cut two 18¼" x 18¼" (47 x 47cm) squares. Then, crosscut them diagonally twice for 8 quarter-square side triangles.

3. Cut two 9⅜" x 9⅜" (24 x 24cm) squares. Then, crosscut them diagonally once for 4 half-square corner triangles.

ASSEMBLY

Lay out the top with the blocks on point. Then, place the side triangles and corner triangles. Sew the pieces together, making diagonal rows. Sew the rows together. Trim the quilt top, if needed, leaving a ¼" (0.5cm) seam allowance all around.

Quilt Top Assembly

BORDERS

Make 96 Flying Geese units and 24 Half-Square Triangle units, using the instructions from the Beach Glass Quilt project (see page 26). Sew together 4 Flying Geese units with 1 Half-Square Triangle unit. Sew 6 of each of these units together end to end for each border, as shown. Sew the borders to the quilt top.

FINISHING

1. Mark the quilt top using a design of your choice.

2. Layer the quilt top with the batting and backing; baste it in place.

3. Quilt as desired, and then bind the edges.

4. Add a label, and sign, date, and photograph your finished quilt.

Border Strip

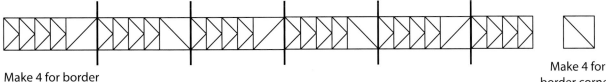

Make 4 for border

Make 4 for border corners

Sand Treasures Wall Hanging or Table Topper

DIMENSIONS: 21½" x 21½" (55 x 55cm)

This project incorporates an embroidery version of the appliqué patterns on the four center squares.

Project Directions

1. Cut four 6½" x 6½" (16.5 x 16.5cm) squares. Trace an embroidery design at the center of each square, and embroider it. Note: You may want to cut out the squares after completing the embroidery work to accommodate the hoop.

2. Make 16 Flying Geese units, using the instructions from the Beach Glass Quilt project (see page 26).

3. Cut one 3½" x 3½" (9 x 9cm) square for the center.

4. Assemble in rows; then sew the rows together.

BORDER

Cut four 3½" x 25" (9 x 63.5cm) strips from the border fabric. Sew the borders on and make mitered corners. See Mitered Corners on page 126 for more information.

Quick Seaside Project: Sand Treasures Hot Pad

DIMENSIONS: 10" x 10" (25.5 x 25.5cm)

Why not use the odds and ends you might have left over from the Sand Treasures Quilt project to make a hot pad? Use this to practice the raw-edge appliqué technique (see page 130) and machine quilting.

Seaside Style: Driftwood Fish

Collecting driftwood is one of the simple pleasures of going for a walk on the beach. It is an activity that family members of all ages can enjoy, and creating an art project from the collected wood brings this experience full circle.

Project Directions

1. Lay out the driftwood until your imagination has created a fish!

2. Use a small drill to place 2 holes in each piece of driftwood wide enough to accommodate craft wire or a piece of rope.

3. As you thread the wire through the driftwood, add beads between pieces to keep the wood separated.

4. To finish the project, twist the extra wire into a loop for hanging the fish.

5. The driftwood can be sealed with polyurethane. Make sure it is totally dry before hanging the project on the wall.

Good Neighbors & Best Friends Wall Hanging or Table Runner

DIMENSIONS: 21½" x 47½" (54.5 x 120.5cm)

Weather notwithstanding, the morning porch beckons best friends and neighbors. It receives sunlight yearlong, and the storefront door is etched with a welcoming quilt basket and spaced square border motif. This project celebrates this gathering place and all the memories that are created there.

The wall hanging is a combination of three Best Friend blocks and four Good Neighbor blocks. This project is the perfect size for a table runner...a wonderful house warming, hostess, or thank you gift.

Fabric Requirements

- ☐ 1 yd. (100cm) floral print for blocks, border, and binding
- ☐ ⅔ yd. (67cm) solid fabric for blocks and border
- ☐ ½ yd. (50cm) white for blocks
- ☐ Batting and backing

This design is etched on the door to Beckie's porch—a favorite gathering place for friends and family. The design features the same Half-Square Triangle units used in the blocks for the quilt.

Cutting & Sewing Directions

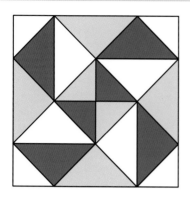

6. Make 16 half-square corner triangles by cutting eight 2⅜" x 2⅜" (6 x 6cm) squares from the white. Crosscut the squares diagonally once.

7. Lay out each block, and sew as illustrated. Make 4 blocks. Trim to 6½" (16.5cm).

1. Cut two 3⅜" x 3⅜" (11 x 11cm) squares from both the floral print and solid fabrics. Then crosscut the squares twice diagonally.

2. Make 4 Quarter-Square Triangle units as shown above for the block center.

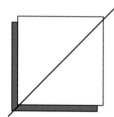 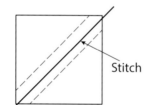 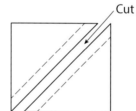

Cut

Stitch

3. Make 16 Half-Square Triangle units by cutting eight 3" x 3" (7.5 x 7.5cm) squares from both the solid and white fabrics.

4. Layer the solid squares and white squares with right sides together; then draw a diagonal line from corner to corner. Stitch ¼" (0.5cm) on each side of the drawn line. Cut the squares apart on the diagonal line. Press the seam to the dark side.

5. Make 16 quarter-square side triangles by cutting four 4¼" x 4¼" (11 x 11cm) squares from the floral print. Crosscut the squares diagonally twice.

1. Cut two 2" (5cm)-wide strips, selvage to selvage, from the white and floral fabrics. Layer the fabric right sides together, and sew a seam on the long edge. Press the seam to the dark side. Cut the strip into 2" (5cm) segments. Sew into a four-patch.

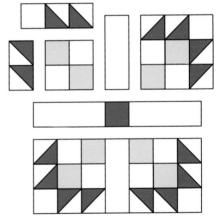

2. Cut two 2⅜" (6cm)-wide strips, selvage to selvage, from the white and solid fabrics. Cut these strips into 2⅜" (6cm) squares. You will need 24 squares from each fabric. Make Half-Square Triangle units following Step 4 for the Good Neighbor block (see page 45).

3. Cut two 2" (5cm)-wide strips, selvage to selvage, from the white fabric. From these strips, cut 12 squares, each 2" x 2" (5 x 5cm), and 12 rectangles, each 2" x 5" (5 x 12.5cm).

4. Cut 3 squares, each 2" x 2" (5 x 5cm), from the solid fabric for the center square.

5. Lay out each block as shown. Make 3 blocks, and trim them to 11" x 11" (28 x 28cm).

This assembly is a little tricky, but the well-crafted results are stunning. The blocks have a border of solid fabric with the floral fabric set into the edges, making the center motif float.

1. Cut four 1½" (4cm)-wide strips, selvage to selvage, from the solid fabric. Cut these strips into eight 1½" x 5" (4 x 12.5cm) pieces and four 1½" x 12½" (4 x 32cm) pieces. Also cut 8 strips, each 1½" x 7½" (4 x 19cm).

2. Cut four 5" x 6½" (12.5 x 16.5cm) rectangles, two 5" x 9" (12.5 x 23cm) rectangles, two 1½" x 5" (4 x 12.5cm) strips, and one 9" x 9" (23 x 23cm) square from floral print. Crosscut the square diagonally once.

3. Cut one 1½" (4cm)-wide strip, selvage to selvage, from the floral print for the outer border.

4. Sew a 1½" x 5" (4 x 12.5cm) solid strip to each 5" x 6½" (12.5 x 16.5cm) floral rectangle (makes 4).

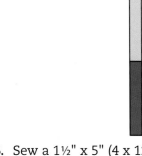

5. Sew a 1½" x 5" (4 x 12.5cm) solid strip to each 1½" x 5" (4 x 12.5cm) floral strip (makes 2).

6. Sew a 1½" x 5" (4 x 12.5cm) solid strip to each 5" x 9" (12.5 x 23cm) floral rectangle (makes 2).

7. Sew the 1½" x 12½" (4 x 32cm) solid border strips on 2 sides of the top and bottom Best Friend blocks.

Section 1

Section 2

Section 3

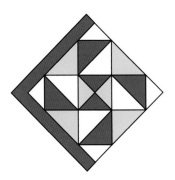

8. Sew the 1½" x 7½" (4 x 19cm) solid border strips on 2 sides of each of the 4 Good Neighbor blocks. Note: Mitering the corners is nice but not necessary.

9. Lay out the pieces, and sew them into 3 sections following the diagram on page 48.

10. Once the top is assembled, trim the sides so there is a space of 1½" (4cm) from the Good Neighbor blocks to the outside edge and 2½" (6.5cm) from the Best Friend blocks to the outside edge.

11. The final step is to sew the 1½" (4cm) floral fabric strips to the top and bottom points.

FINISHING

1. Mark the top with your favorite quilting design.

2. Layer the top, batting, and backing; baste all 3 layers together.

3. Quilt and bind the project.

4. Sign, date, and photograph your finished quilt.

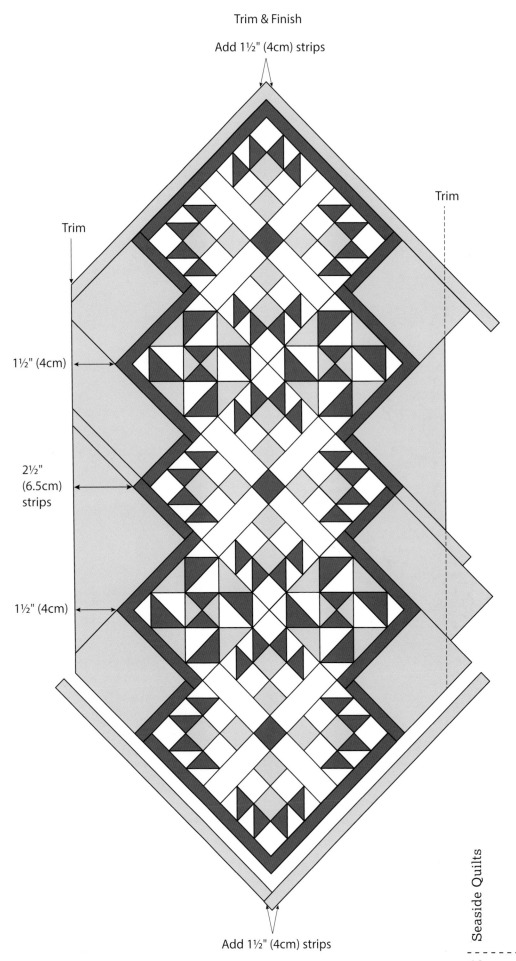

Trim & Finish

Add 1½" (4cm) strips

Trim

Trim

1½" (4cm)

2½" (6.5cm) strips

1½" (4cm)

Add 1½" (4cm) strips

Seaside Quilts

Seaside Style: Fabric-Wrapped and Coiled Tray

Beckie created this centerpiece tray for the luncheon table out of fabric strips and cording. It is so much fun to make a basket that will tie your entire theme together. Lots of leftover scraps from completed projects and a few new pieces from projects not yet started are all that's needed to create this tray.

Leftover fabric from other seaside projects and some cotton cording can be used to create the perfect tray or bowl for a beach-themed kitchen.

Supplies

- ☐ ¾" (2cm)-diameter 100% cotton cording
- ☐ ½"–¾" (1.5–2cm)-wide fabric strips

Project Directions

CUTTING A CONTINUOUS FABRIC STRIP

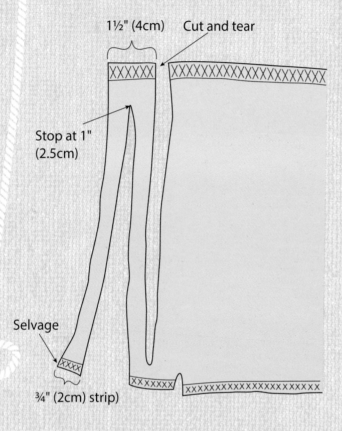

1½" (4cm)   Cut and tear

Stop at 1" (2.5cm)

Selvage

¾" (2cm) strip)

1. Tear fabric strips ½"–¾" (1.5–2cm) wide.

2. For a continuous strip, make a small cut on the selvage, ¾" (2cm) from the edge. Tear the fabric from this point to 1" (2.5cm) before the next selvage edge. Measure 1½" (4cm) along the new selvage edge. Make a cut, and tear the fabric to within 1" (2.5cm) before the next selvage edge. Repeat this process for a continuous strip.

3. To join the strips, cut a slit in the end of the working strip, about 1" (2.5cm) from the end. Do the same with the new strip. Lay the strip ends on top of each other with the slits lined up and the tails going in opposite directions. Insert the new strip through the slit in the working strip. Then, bring the tail of the new strip through the slit in the new strip and pull.

Cut a slit 1"(2.5cm) from selvage edge

New strip

JOINING STRIPS

Working strip

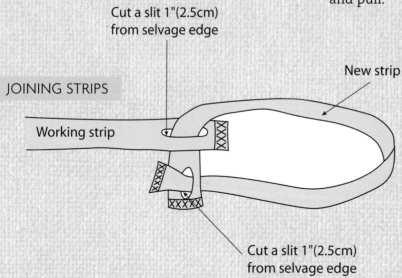

Cut a slit 1"(2.5cm) from selvage edge

CONSTRUCTION

The shape of the basket is determined by how you choose to form the base (round, rectangular, or oval). The height of the sides will determine whether it is a bowl or tray.

1. Place your fabric strip about 2" (5cm) from the end of the cord. Hold the fabric in place with a Clover Wonder Clip or a piece of tape.

2. Wrap the fabric strip tightly around the cord. Hold the fabric at an angle so the wrap is diagonal and overlaps the edge of the previous wrap as you go.

3. Continue wrapping for approximately 12" (30.5cm). Hold the fabric in place with a clip or tape at this point.

4. Form the covered cord into the shape you want for the bottom of your tray or bowl by coiling it into the desired shape.

5. Continue wrapping the exposed cording in the fabric, but now, every 3 or 4 wraps, take the fabric under and then over the previous coiled row to secure the coil in place and form the shape. Note: If you use a fabric with a noticeably lighter reverse side, you may want to twist the fabric to the right side as you work.

6. Continue wrapping the cord, coiling and securing it until the piece is the size and shape you want. Note: If a large project is your goal, add a stabilizing wire as you coil for additional support.

7. When she was happy with the shape and size of her project, Beckie continued to cover the remaining excess cord and integrated it into the design of the finished piece.

Seaside Serenade

DIMENSIONS: 92" x 93" (233.5 x 236cm)

The centerpiece of this quilt is a glorious bouquet of shells, coral, and seaweed leaves, all gathered in an elegant two-tone vase. It is as if the birds, wind, and ocean especially delivered this bouquet in celebration of gifts from the sea. The outermost blocks are Birds in the Air. They seem to be flying with the Northwind blocks above the border of the wave-like block called Nautilus...all in an extraordinary Seaside Serenade.

The colors in this quilt range from peach to russet and from soft to dark green, with a lovely off-white and floral background. A special feature is the pile of shells appliquéd onto the corners at the bottom of the quilt. The mood of this quilt is light and inviting and oh so cozy on cool fall and winter nights.

Fabric Requirements

- ☐ 2½ yd. (250cm) total of assorted soft peach to russet values
- ☐ 1½ yd. (150cm) total of assorted soft to medium-dark greens
- ☐ ½ yd. (50cm) dark green for outer border and corners
- ☐ 4¼ yd. (425cm) background
- ☐ Assorted colors and textures for appliqué
- ☐ 2 yd. (200cm) medium-weight non-fusible interfacing
- ☐ ⅝ yd. (62.5cm) binding
- ☐ Batting and backing

G. LILEY

Cutting & Sewing Directions

BIRDS IN THE AIR BLOCK

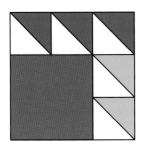

Trim to 10½" (26.5)

1. Cut one 7⅛" x 7⅛" (18 x 18cm) square from the russet fabric.

2. Cut three 4¼" x 4¼" (11 x 11cm) squares from the background and 3 squares of the same size from assorted greens. Make 5 Half-Square Triangle units (see page 29). Trim the squares to 3⅞" (10cm).

Row 1

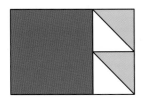

Row 2

3. Sew 3 of the Half-Square Triangle units together to form Row 1. Sew 2 Half-Square Triangle units together; then sew them onto the large square, making Row 2. Sew the rows together. Make 20 blocks. Trim them to 10½" (26.5cm).

NORTHWIND BLOCK

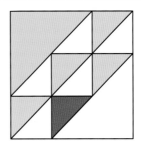

Trim to 10½" (26.5)

1. Cut one 7¼" x 7¼" (18.5 x 18.5cm) square from the background and 1 square of the same size from a medium peach fabric. Then, crosscut the squares diagonally once from corner to corner. You need 1 triangle of each color for the block.

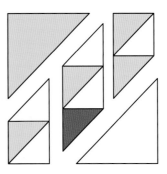

2. Cut three 4¼" x 4¼" (11 x 11cm) squares from the background and 3 squares of the same size from assorted peach fabrics. Then, crosscut the squares diagonally once from corner to corner. Make 3 Half-Square Triangle units, and add the remaining triangles as shown.

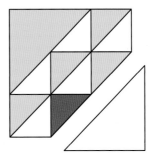

3. Sew the triangle units together, forming a diagonal row. Then, add the large triangles to each side. Make 16 blocks. Trim them to 10½" (26.5cm).

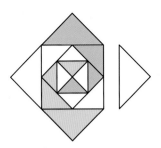

1. Cut one 3¾" x 3¾" (9.5 x 9.5cm) square from a peach fabric and a green fabric and 1 square of the same size from the background fabric. Then, crosscut the squares twice diagonally, creating quarter-square triangles. Lay out a square with 1 peach triangle and 1 green triangle across from each other and 2 background triangles across from each other. Sew this block into a Quarter-Square Triangle unit. The extra pieces will be used to form other squares.

2. Cut 1 peach, 1 green, and 1 background square, each 2¾" x 2¾" (7 x 7cm). Then, crosscut the squares diagonally once. Sew the peach triangle ¼ turn to the left of the first peach triangle. Sew the green triangle opposite the peach, and sew the 2 background triangles on the remaining opposing sides. Trim to 3⅝" (9cm).

3. Cut 1 peach, 1 green, and 1 background square, each 3½" x 3½" (9 x 9cm). Then, crosscut the squares diagonally once. Sew a peach triangle ¼ turn to the left of the previous peach triangle. Sew the green triangle opposite the peach, and sew the 2 background triangles on the remaining opposing sides. Trim to 5" (12.5cm). Continue with this pattern for all the following steps.

4. Continue the pattern using 4½" x 4½" (11.5 x 11.5cm) squares crosscut diagonally once. Sew the triangles to the block as in Step 3. Trim to 7" (18cm).

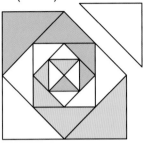

Trim to 10½" (26.5cm)

5. Finish the pattern using 5⅞" x 5⅞" (15 x 15cm) squares crosscut diagonally once. Sew the triangles as in Step 3. Make 12 blocks. Trim them to 10½" (26.5cm).

APPLIQUÉ

1. Follow the directions for Off-Quilt Appliqué on page 128.

2. Make 1 center bouquet.

3. Make 1 corner appliqué piece and 1 in reverse.

QUILT TOP ASSEMBLY

1. Cut one 22" x 22" (56 x 56cm) square from the background fabric.

2. Cut four 11" x 22" (28 x 56cm) rectangles from the background fabric.

3. Cut four 18¼" x 18¼" (48 x 48cm) squares from a medium green fabric. Then, crosscut the squares diagonally twice, making quarter-square triangles for the quilt sides, top, and bottom.

4. Cut two 18" x 18" (45.5 x 45.5cm) squares from a dark green fabric. Then, crosscut them diagonally once to form the 4 quilt corners.

5. Lay out the blocks and pieces, and sew them together in diagonal rows as shown. Sew the rows together.

6. Set the center bouquet and corner appliqué pieces in place, and sew them to the quilt top.

BORDER

Cut nine 2" (5cm)-wide strips, selvage to selvage, from the dark green. Sew the borders onto both sides of the quilt, and the top and bottom.

FINISHING

1. Mark the quilt top using a design of your choice.

2. Layer the quilt top with the batting and backing; baste it in place.

3. Quilt as desired, and then bind the edges.

4. Add a label, and sign, date, and photograph your finished quilt.

Quilt Top Assembly

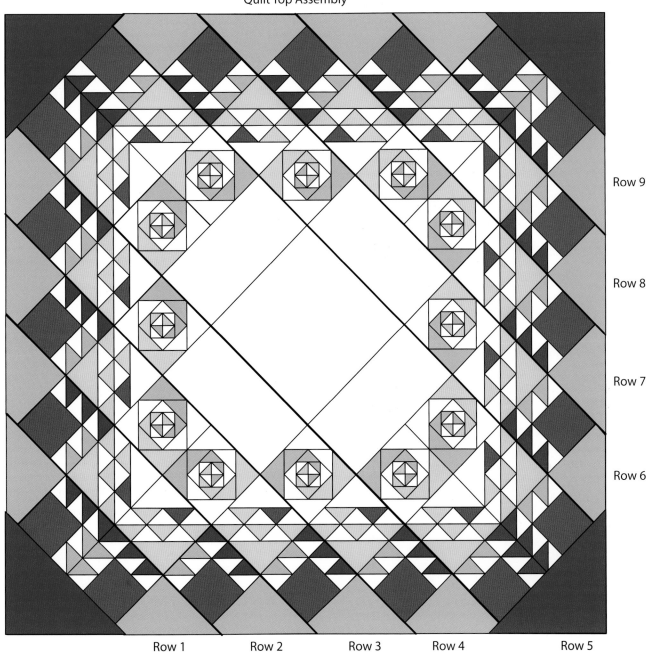

Row 9

Row 8

Row 7

Row 6

Row 1   Row 2   Row 3   Row 4   Row 5

Seaside Quilts

Seaside Bounty Wall Quilt

DIMENSIONS: 34" x 42½" (86.5 x 108cm)

This wall hanging focuses on the basket centerpiece, filled with the bounty from the sea. It's a brilliant spot of color during the winter months at the beach and brings family beachcombing memories to mind with a smile. The background fabric is a horizontal striation of blues and greens reminiscent of the ocean.

Fabric Requirements

- [ ] 29" x 41" (73.5 x 104cm) background
- [ ] 1 yd. (100cm) total of assorted peaches and blues for border
- [ ] Assorted colors and textures for appliqué
- [ ] Fusible web (we recommend Lite Steam-A-Seam 2)
- [ ] Pressing sheet (we recommend Teflon's)
- [ ] Mini-iron (we recommend Clover Needlecraft Incorporated's)
- [ ] Bent-tip scissors
- [ ] Paper scissors
- [ ] Ironing board and iron
- [ ] 1½ yd. (150cm) binding and backing
- [ ] Batting

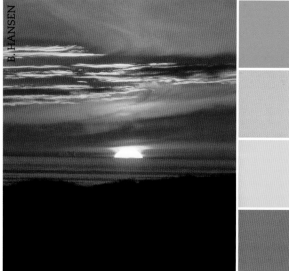

The pieced outer border, made from scraps of blues and peaches, reflects gorgeous beach sunsets.

Cutting & Sewing Directions

APPLIQUÉ

The appliqué for this project uses a satin stitch, which, when using a 40-weight rayon thread, leaves a hint of a shine. The width of the stitch depends on the size of the appliqué shell. You may find you need to reduce the width of the stitch as the shell tapers. The appliqué can also be sewn with a small zigzag or hem stitch using invisible thread.

1. Tracing the patterns for the appliqué pieces directly onto the fusible web will create a reverse image of the pattern. If you wish the appliqué to appear as shown in the project photo, first trace the pattern from the back side over a light box or window.

2. Trace each appliqué piece on the fusible web, numbering each piece with a pencil and leaving the dotted overlap lines. Using paper scissors, rough cut the pieces from the fusible web, cutting outside the pattern lines. Press the fusible web pieces onto the desired fabric following manufacturer's directions. Then, cut the pieces from the fabric by cutting along the pattern lines, including the overlap lines.

3. You can attach your appliqué pieces directly to your quilt background fabric or press them onto a pressing sheet and release them when all are done. Adding the pieces to a pressing sheet first allows you to try different fabric choices and placement before adding the appliqué to your quilt background. To do this, place your pattern on an ironing surface, put the pressing sheet over the pattern, and lay out the appliqué pieces, starting with Piece 1. Remove the backing paper from the overlap or the entire back of Piece 2, and place it in its position. Press the overlap with a mini-iron. Continue this process, placing the appliqué pieces in numerical order and moving the pressing sheet as necessary.

The pieces will release from the sheet when you are finished. Make sure the sheet is always behind the piece you are pressing.

4. Attach the appliqué pieces to your quilt top and topstitch the edges using a satin stitch.

5. When the appliqué is complete, press the entire quilt top and then trim it to 27½" x 39" (70 x 99cm).

BORDER

1. Cut twenty-three 4⅜" x 4⅜" (11 x 11cm) squares from each assorted peach and blue fabric.

2. Layer a peach and blue square with right sides together, and draw a line diagonally from corner to corner.

3. Stitch ¼" (0.5cm) on both sides of the drawn line. Then cut along the diagonal line. The yield is 2 Half-Square Triangle units. Make 46 units. Trim them to 4" (10cm).

4. Lay out and stitch the border squares in 2 strips of 14 squares for each side and 2 strips of 9 squares each for the top and bottom. Press the strips after stitching.

5. Attach the borders to the quilt top, and press.

FINISHING

1. Mark the quilt top using a design of your choice.

2. Layer the quilt top with the batting and backing; baste it in place.

3. Quilt as desired, and then bind the edges.

4. Add a label, and sign, date, and photograph your finished quilt.

Blue & White Colorwash Irish Chain

DIMENSIONS: 72" x 90" (183 x 228.5cm), sized to fit a twin-size bed

Washing color across a quilt surface is all about tonal values. You can see this happen at the shoreline as shallow ocean waves move across the sand in foaming shades of blue and gray and tan and white. In the dunes, notice how many shades of yellow and green you can see in the grasses rooted there. In years past, Carol designed and sold this quilt pattern. One of eighteen, this color scheme proved the most popular and enduring.

The blue and white colors used in this quilt are reminiscent of blue and white ocean waves.

Fabric Requirements

- ☐ 1¼ yd. (125cm) background
- ☐ ½ yd. (50cm) Color 1, light print
- ☐ ½ yd. (50cm) Color 2, light/medium print
- ☐ ½ yd. (50cm) Color 3, medium print
- ☐ ¾ yd. (75cm) Color 4, light/dark print
- ☐ ¾ yd. (75cm) Color 5, dark print
- ☐ ¾ yd. (75cm) Color 6, light/dark print
- ☐ ¾ yd. (75cm) Color 7, medium print
- ☐ ¾ yd. (75cm) Color 8, light/medium print
- ☐ ½ yd. (50cm) Color 9, light print
- ☐ ½ yd. (50cm) Border 1, dark blue
- ☐ 1½ yd. (150cm) Border 2, blue and white floral
- ☐ 5 yd. (500cm) backing
- ☐ ¾ yd. (75cm) binding
- ☐ Batting

Selecting Fabrics

When choosing the fabrics for this quilt, keep in mind that medium- to small-scale prints work best. Tiny prints (calicos) read as solids, and large-scale prints when cut to 2½" (6.5cm) may completely lose the value you need. For a seamless blend, Fabrics 1 and 9 need to have the same color background as the fabric used in the large block areas. Background fabrics do not have to be solid and can have a very open print or texture.

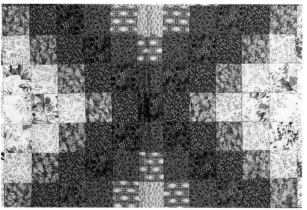

Cutting & Sewing Directions

PREPARATION

From the background fabric:

1. Cut two 2½" (6.5cm)-wide strips, selvage to selvage. Then, cut the strips into thirty-one 2½" x 2½" (6.5 x 6.5cm) squares.

2. Cut four 2½" (64mm)-wide strips, selvage to selvage. Then, cut the strips into twenty-four 2½" x 6½" (6.5 x 16.5cm) rectangles.

3. Cut six 10½" x 10½" (26.5 x 26.5cm) squares.

From Fabrics 1–9:
Cut the following strips selvage to selvage, 2½" (6.5cm) wide. Place the fabric number on the stack of strips for easy identification when it comes time to sew the strips together.

- Fabric 1: Cut 5 strips
- Fabric 2: Cut 6 strips
- Fabric 3: Cut 7 strips
- Fabric 4: Cut 8 strips
- Fabric 5: Cut 8 strips
- Fabric 6: Cut 8 strips
- Fabric 7: Cut 8 strips
- Fabric 8: Cut 8 strips
- Fabric 9: Cut 7 strips

This chart shows all of the blocks' pieced units and the quantities of each.

FABRIC COLOR	QUANTITY
#1	8 squares
#1-2	8 pieced units
#1-2-3	8 pieced units
#1-2-3-4	14 pieced units
#1-2-3-4-5	17 pieced units
#2-3-4-5	5 pieced units
#2-3-4-5-6	20 pieced units
#3-4-5-6	4 pieced units
#3-4-5-6-7	20 pieced units
#4-5-6-7	4 pieced units
#4-5-6-7-8	22 pieced units
#5-6-7-8	4 pieced units
#5-6-7-8-9	22 pieced units
#6-7-8-9	20 pieced units
#7-8-9	16 pieced units
#8-9	16 pieced units
#9	12 squares

SEWING STRATA AND CUTTING UNITS

Cutting strata units

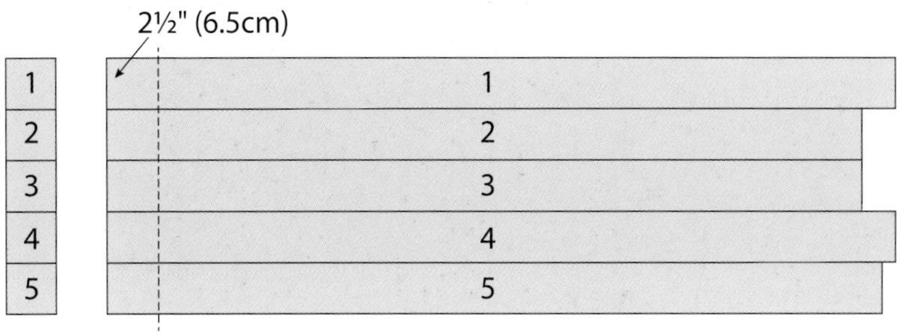

2½" (6.5cm)

For speed and ease in assembling this Irish Chain, we are recommending the strip piecing method. The strips will be sewn into a strata and then cut into units that are used to create blocks. The blocks are then sewn together into the quilt top. A reminder: Use an even ¼" (0.5cm) seam allowance along the entire side of the strips. When you are finished sewing, press the strata and make sure there is no buckling at the seam. Cut the strata into 2½" (6.5cm) units following the chart below, and label the stacks according to the chart.

Once all the units are cut out and the stacks are clearly labeled, you can begin to assemble the blocks. Lay out each block as shown. Blank squares and rectangles represent the background units already cut. Press the seams so each row opposes the next for easy and accurate sewing.

ASSEMBLY

Lay out the blocks, and sew them in rows. Then, sew the rows together, making sure all seams oppose each other.

BORDERS

1. From Border Fabric 1, cut seven 1½" (4cm)-wide strips, by the width of the fabric.

2. From Border Fabric 2, cut seven 6½" (16.5cm)-wide strips by the width of the fabric.

3. Sew the border strips together end to end to match the measurements needed for each side of the quilt. Sew the borders to the quilt top, mitering the corners. See Mitered Corners on page 126 for more information.

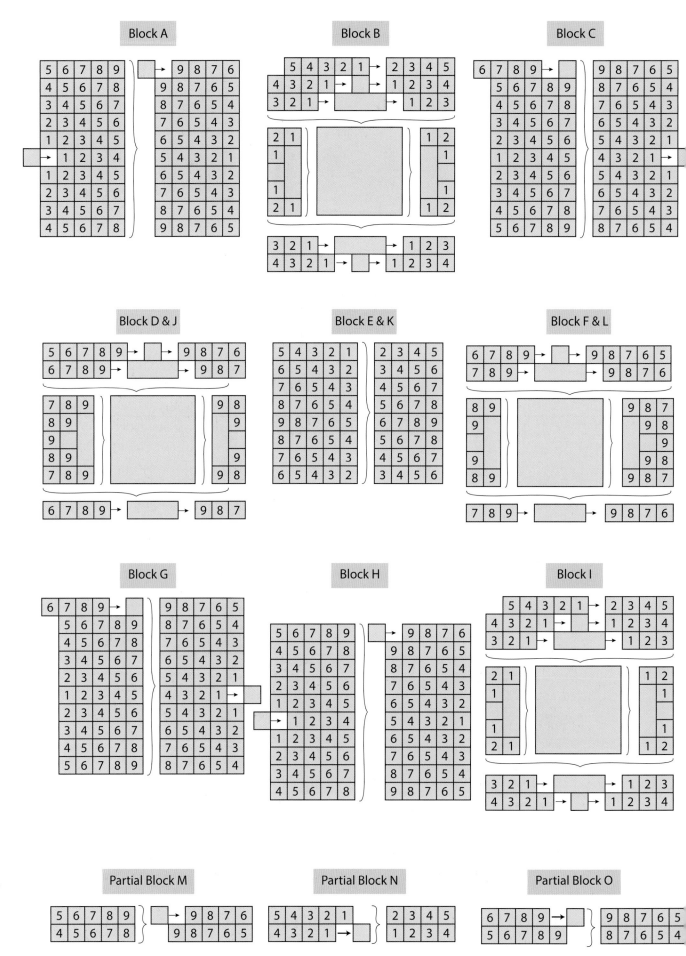

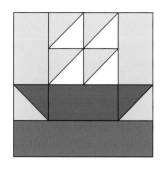 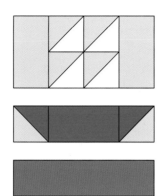 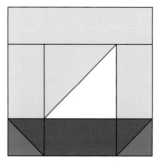 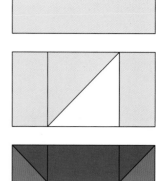

Cutting & Sewing Directions

SHIP BLOCK

1. Cut two 2½" x 4½" (6.5 x 21.5cm) rectangles and three 2⅞" (7.5cm) squares from the blue sky fabric.

2. Cut two 2⅞" (7.5cm) squares from white fabric for the sails.

3. Cut one 2½" x 4½" (6.5 x 11.5cm) rectangle and one 2⅞" (7.5cm) square from red for the boat.

4. Cut one 2½" x 8½" (6.5 x 21.5cm) strip from turquoise fabric for the water.

5. Makes two stacks of 1 blue square and 1 white square each, right sides together. Draw a diagonal line from corner to corner on each set of squares. Then, stitch ¼" (0.5cm) on each side of the diagonal line. Cut each set of squares on the diagonal line, and press each unit open with the seam pressed to the darker fabric. Repeat this process with 1 blue square and 1 red square, right sides together. The yield will be 4 blue and white Half-Square Triangle units and 2 blue and red Half-Square Triangle units. Trim the units to 2½" (6.5cm).

6. Following the illustration, lay out the block pieces and sew them into rows. Then, sew the rows together to form the full block, pressing the seams in opposite directions. Trim the block to 8½" (21.5cm). Make 3 blocks.

SAILBOAT BLOCK

1. Cut one 2½" x 8½" (6.5 x 21.5cm) strip, two 2½" x 4½" (6.5 x 11.5cm) rectangles, and one 4⅞" (12.5cm) square from the blue sky fabric.

2. Cut one 4⅞" (12.5cm) square from white fabric for the sail.

3. Cut one 2½" x 4½" (6.5 x 11.5cm) rectangle and one 2⅞" (7.5cm) square from the blue boat fabric.

4. Cut one 2⅞" (7.5cm) square from turquoise fabric for the water.

5. Layer the blue (sky) and white 4⅞" (12.5cm) squares right sides together. Then, layer the blue (boat) and turquoise 2⅞" (7.5cm) squares right sides together. Draw a diagonal line from corner to corner on each set of squares. Then, stitch ¼" (0.5cm) on each side of the diagonal lines. Cut each set of squares on the diagonal line, and press each unit open with the seam pressed to the darker fabric. Trim the large square to 4½" (11.5cm) and the small squares to 2½" (6.5cm).

6. Following the illustration, lay out the block pieces and sew them into rows. Then, sew the rows together to form the full block, pressing the seams in opposite directions. Trim the block to 8½" (21.5cm). Make 3 blocks.

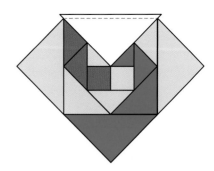

Note: The wave block is made from four different fabrics and values. Plan the color placement before cutting. You will be making four blocks.

1. Cut four 2" x 2" (5 x 5cm) squares from each of the 4 fabrics selected for the wave blocks. Using 1 square from each color, make a four-patch.

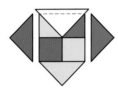

2. Cut one 4¼" x 4¼" (11 x 11cm) square from each of the 4 fabrics. Crosscut the squares diagonally twice from corner to corner. Sew 1 quarter-square triangle of each color onto the four-patch in the order shown.

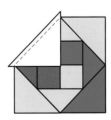

3. Cut one 3⅞" x 3⅞" (10 x 10cm) square from each of the 4 fabrics. Crosscut the squares diagonally twice from corner to corner. Following the order shown in the illustration, sew 1 quarter-square triangle of each color onto the unit made in Step 2.

4. Cut one 7¼" x 7¼" (18.5 x 18.5cm) square from each of the 4 fabrics. Crosscut the squares diagonally twice from corner to corner. Following the order shown in the illustration, sew 1 quarter-square triangle of each color onto the unit made in Step 3.

5. Cut one 6⅞" x 6⅞" (17.5 x 17.5cm) square from each of the 4 fabrics. Crosscut the squares diagonally twice from corner to corner. Following the order shown in the illustration, sew 1 quarter-square triangle of each color onto the unit made in Step 4. Cutting the fabric in this manner will yield enough triangles to make 4 blocks.

6. Sew the 4 blocks together in a row. The row should measure 12½" x 48½" (32 x 123.5cm). Adjust the joining seams if needed.

ASSEMBLY

1. Sew the 3 Ship and 3 Sailboat blocks together in a row, alternating the blocks. This row should measure 8½" x 48½" (21.5 x 123.5cm). Adjust joining seams if needed.

2. For the sky, cut a 15" x 48½" (38 x 123.5cm) segment from the sky blue fabric and sew it to the top of the Ship and Sailboat pieced strip.

3. For the water (fish background), cut an 8½" x 48½" (21.5 x 123.5cm) segment from the water background for fish fabric

and sew it to the bottom of the Ship and Sailboat pieced strip. Sew the Waves pieced strip to the bottom of the water (fish background) strip.

4. For the water (below waves), cut a 6 ½" x 48½" (16.5 x 123.5cm) segment from the water for below waves fabric and sew it to the bottom of the Waves pieced block.

5. For the rocks, cut a 3" x 48½" (7.5 x 123.5cm) segment from the rock fabric and sew it to the bottom of the water (below waves) strip.

6. For the sand, cut a 20" x 48½" (51 x 123.5cm) segment from the sand fabric and sew it to the bottom of the rocks strip.

APPLIQUÉ

Now the fun begins! Using the patterns on pages 134–137 and following the off-quilt appliqué technique on page 128, make the items listed below for appliqué. Then, using the photo for reference, position and appliqué all pieces onto the quilt.

- Sun: Make 1
- Kites: Make 3
- Fish: Make 2 of Fish 1, make 1 of Fish 2 and 1 of Fish 2 in reverse, and make 1 of Fish 3
- Pails: Make 5 (1 with handle up)
- Ball: Make 1
- Crab: Make 1
- Grass: Make 1 full of A, make 1 half of A, and make 2 of B

BORDERS

1. Cut eight 4" (10cm)-wide strips, selvage to selvage.

2. Measure the quilt sides; then sew enough strips together to equal the length, joining the strips end to end. Sew the side borders to the quilt top.

3. Measure the top and bottom of the quilt top, including the side borders just added. Sew enough strips to equal this measurement; join strips end to end if needed. Sew the top and bottom borders to the quilt top.

FINISHING

1. Mark the quilt top using a design of your choice.

2. Layer the quilt top with the batting and backing; baste it in place.

3. Quilt as desired, and then bind the edges.

4. Add a label, and sign, date, and photograph your finished quilt.

Quilt Top Assembly

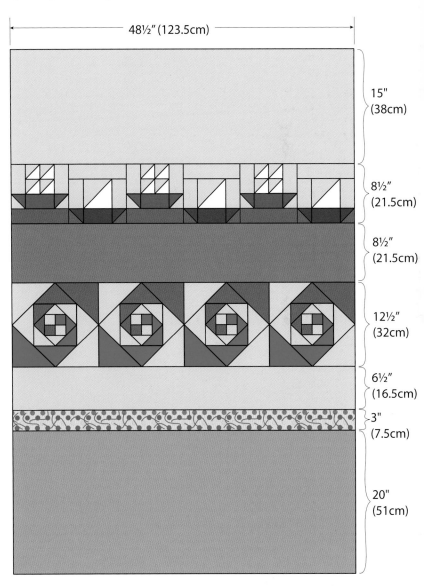

48½" (123.5cm)

15" (38cm)

8½" (21.5cm)

8½" (21.5cm)

12½" (32cm)

6½" (16.5cm)

3" (7.5cm)

20" (51cm)

A Day at the Beach Growth Chart

DIMENSIONS: 20¾" x 60¼" (52.5 x 153cm)

What a fun way to watch your beach babies grow! Place this chart on the wall exactly 24" (61cm) from the floor. Use a permanent pen to mark the date and your child's height. You can even add keepsake pockets for pictures and special notes.

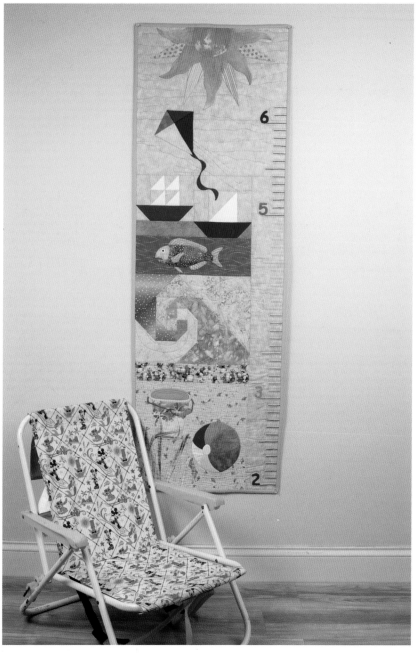

Fabric Requirements

- ☐ ⅝ yd. (62.5cm) blue background for sky, boat blocks, and ruler

- ☐ I fat quarter (45.5 x 56cm) fabric for rocks

- ☐ I fat quarter (45.5 x 56cm) fabric for sand

- ☐ I fat quarter (45.5 x 56cm) fabric for grass

- ☐ 6–7 fat quarters (45.5 x 56cm) light to medium values of aqua for wave block, boat blocks, fish background, ball, and pail.

- ☐ Scraps or ⅛ yd. (12.5cm) for all of the following fabrics:

  Solids: Red, white, blue, yellow, green, and orange

  Prints: Yellow/orange (sun), batik and lavender (fish), novelty print (pail)

- ☐ Embroidery Floss DMC Red #321, Yellow #973, Orange #947, Green #700, and Blue #798

- ☐ I yd. (100cm) medium-weight, no-iron interfacing for appliqué and pockets

- ☐ Scraps for keepsake pockets (optional)

- ☐ Grosgrain ribbon for keepsake pockets (optional)

- ☐ 3½" x 3½" (9 x 9cm) clear vinyl squares for picture pocket (optional)

- ☐ Backing, binding, and batting

Tip

You may have much of the fabric needed for this project left over from making the quilt. Remember to check your scraps!

Cutting & Sewing Directions

1. Cut a 19" x 20½" (48.5 x 52cm) rectangle from the sky fabric.

2. Make 1 Ship block and 1 Sailboat block following the instructions for the Day at the Beach Quilt (see page 80). Sew the 2 blocks together. Trim them to 8½" x 16½" (21.5 x 43cm).

3. Cut a 5½" x 16½" (14 x 42cm) rectangle from the water fabric and appliqué 1 Fish onto it. If desired, you can assemble the quilt top first and then add the appliqué.

4. Make 1 Wave block following the instructions for the Day at the Beach Quilt (see page 80). Trim the block to 12½" (32cm).

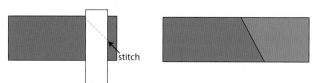

5. For the pieced unit (filler), use colors that match the Wave block to cut one 5" x 11" (12.5 x 28cm) rectangle and one 5" x 7½" (12.5 x 19cm) rectangle. Join the 2 rectangles end to end by stitching them at a 45° angle. Trim the seam allowance to ¼" (0.5cm). Attach the filler pieced unit to the Wave block. Trim to 12½" x 16½" (32 x 42cm).

6. Cut one 3" x 16½" (7.5 x 42cm) rectangle from the rock fabric.

7. Cut one 14½" x 16½" (37 x 42cm) rectangle from the sand fabric.

8. Cut one 5" x 41½" (12.5 x 105.5cm) strip from the sky fabric.

9. Sew all sections together as illustrated.

APPLIQUÉ

Following the off-quilt appliqué instructions on page 128, and using the patterns on pages 134–138, make the following appliqué designs and attach them to the growth chart. Use the project photo for reference.

- Sun
- Kite
- Fish
- Pail
- Ball
- Partial grass B
- Numbers: 2, 3, 4, 5, and 6

RULER EMBROIDERY

Place the number 2 at the bottom of the chart and carefully measure and mark ruler lines an exact inch (2.5cm) apart. The ruler lines at the numbers are 3" (7.5cm) long, and the remaining lines are 2" (5cm) long. Embroider the ruler lines using a backstitch embroidery stitch.

Quilt Top Assembly

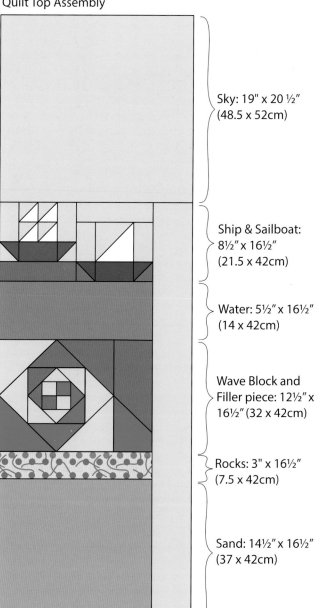

Sky: 19" x 20 ½" (48.5 x 52cm)

Ship & Sailboat: 8½" x 16½" (21.5 x 42cm)

Water: 5½" x 16½" (14 x 42cm)

Wave Block and Filler piece: 12½" x 16½" (32 x 42cm)

Rocks: 3" x 16½" (7.5 x 42cm)

Sand: 14½" x 16½" (37 x 42cm)

Sky: 5" x 41½" (21.5 x 105.5cm)

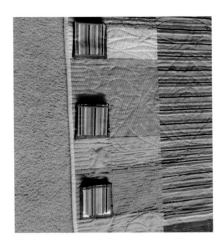

OPTIONAL KEEPSAKE POCKETS

1. To make 1 pocket, cut two 4" x 6½" (10 x 16.5cm) rectangles; one is the pocket front, and the other is the lining.

2. Cut two 4" x 6½" (10 x 16.5cm) rectangles of lightweight interfacing.

3. Cut one 3½" x 3½" (9 x 9cm) square from the clear vinyl (picture pocket).

4. Fuse the interfacing to the wrong sides of the pocket and pocket lining.

5. With right sides together, stitch the sides and top of the pocket. Turn the pocket right side out, and press.

6. Fold the grosgrain ribbon in half over the top of the vinyl square, and stitch it in place.

7. Center the vinyl square on the pocket, and position it ¼" (0.5cm) from the pocket top. Attach the vinyl to the pocket by edge stitching along the sides.

8. Fold grosgrain ribbon over the side edges and bottom of the pocket, and stitch it in place.

9. Pleat the sides to the back of the pocket so that the edge of the ribbon is even with the edge of the vinyl. Stitch the pleats in place along the bottom edge. Make 5 pockets.

10. Hand stitch the pockets to the back of the growth chart.

Turquoise, Green & White Floral Picnic Quilt

DIMENSIONS: 47½" x 71" (123.5 x 180.5cm)

This floral vintage tablecloth (probably from the 1950s) was intact but had a few errant blue spots from the dying process. The dye spots meant it was not in mint condition, but it was just right for the centerpiece of this picnic tablecloth. Washed and pressed, it was clearly meant for a card table. The shape was slightly strange, so before sewing, it was evened up to measure 31½" x 34¾" (80 x 88.5cm).

This vintage tablecloth makes a standout centerpiece for this picnic quilt.

The colors and floral designs on this picnic quilt are reminiscent of some of the unique plants found along the shoreline.

Using Repurposed Linens

A vintage tablecloth is ideal for this project and the one that follows. These tablecloths are easy to find (you or a relative probably own one) and come in sizes from a card table square to a larger rectangle. Here's your opportunity to take it out of storage and make it into the best picnic quilt ever.

Fabric Requirements

FOR TOP:

Use home décor fabric, 54" (137cm) wide

☐ ½ yd. (45.5cm) green for Border 1

☐ ¾ yd. (68.5cm) turquoise dot for Border 2

☐ ⅝ yd.(62.5cm) turquoise and white stripe for Border 3

FOR BACK:

Use standard fabric, 44"–45" (116–116.5cm) wide

☐ ¾ yd. (75cm) stripe fabric

☐ ¾ yd. (75cm) floral fabric

☐ ½ yd. (50cm) white with green dot fabric

☐ ½ yd. (50cm) white with turquoise dot fabric

☐ ½ yd. (50cm) geometric stripe pattern

☐ ½ yd. (50cm) yellow and white print

☐ Binding and batting

This quilt makes a great picnic tablecloth, whether you're eating on the beach or your back porch.

Project Directions

Use a tablecloth or other fabric for one side of the quilt. For the reverse side, cut enough 8½" x 8½" (21.5 x 21.5cm) blocks and 4½" x 8½" (11.5 x 21.5cm) rectangles, which will be used at the beginning and end of alternate rows, to cover the area of the tablecloth or other fabric. Note: Using half of a block at the beginning and ending of one row means the blocks in that row will be offset from the blocks on the next row, and the seams will not match across the rows. This makes a great beginner project.

No border is necessary for this casual picnic quilt, but one could certainly be added to create a larger piece. You can add batting if you want, or just layer, quilt, and bind the front and reverse sides.

Reverse Side Assembly

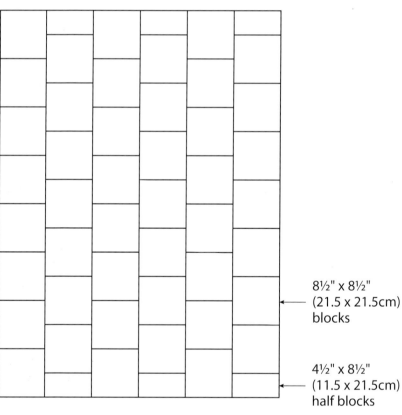

8½" x 8½" (21.5 x 21.5cm) blocks

4½" x 8½" (11.5 x 21.5cm) half blocks

Seaside Style:
Suitcase Picnic Baskets

Refurbished suitcases make great beach picnic baskets! To start out, check the condition and clean the inside and outside of the suitcase you plan to use. Gesso can be used as a primer and will fill any voids on the surface. Paint the suitcase any way you desire. Many hobby stores have decorative painting designs that can be applied to the surface. Add two or three coats of polyurethane to finish and protect the suitcase exterior. The inside can be customized to organize and carry special items secured in pockets or tied in with ribbons.

Supplies

☐ ¼" (0.5cm) Foam Core (cut to the size of the base and lid)

☐ Heavyweight fusible interfacing

☐ Batting

☐ Fiberglass carpet tape

☐ Hot glue gun

☐ Iron

☐ Fabric for lining

☐ Ribbon

Project Directions

Cut the fabric lining, interfacing, and batting 4" (10cm) larger on all sides than the foam core. Iron the interfacing onto the fabric.

FOR THE POCKETS

1. Decide on the height of the pockets for the interior of the suitcase lid. Cut a strip of fabric from selvage to selvage that is double the desired pocket height plus 4" (40cm). Example: Pockets 6" (15cm) high would be cut 12" (30.5cm) + 4" (10cm) = 16" (41cm). Any number of pockets can be worked into this strip of fabric.

2. Cut a piece of interfacing the same height as the pocket fabric by the width of fabric selvage to selvage. Iron the interfacing to the wrong side of the pocket fabric.

3. Determine the number of pockets you want. Then, fold the pocket fabric lengthwise with wrong sides together. Pleat and press the fabric into sections to form the number of pockets desired.

4. Sew ribbon to the inside of the box pleats. This will hold the pockets closed.

5. Align the pocket section with the bottom and left and right edges of the lining fabric for the top of the suitcase. Sew the pocket section in place, stitching between the pockets, along the left and right edges, and along the bottom edge.

LINING THE BASE

Construct the lining for the bottom of the suitcase following the instructions above, but without adding pockets.

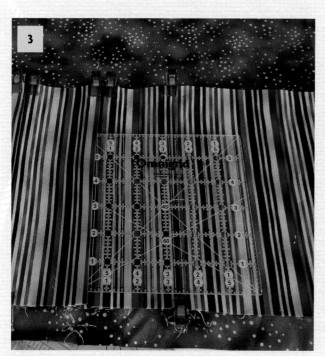

FINISHING

1. For the suitcase lid, place carpet tape along the outer edges of the foam core for the lid as if you were making a frame. Lay the lid lining/pocket section face down, layer the batting on top of it, and then place the foam core on top, with the carpet tape facing up.

2. Remove the protective paper from the carpet tape, exposing the sticky side.

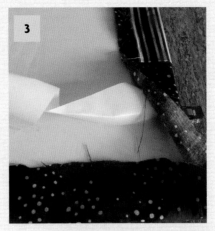

3. Starting at the center of one edge, fold the lining fabric to the back of the foam core and press it in place against the tape. Do the same on the opposite edge, making sure to pull the fabric taut. Work from center out on the remaining sides, stopping about 2" (5cm) from the corners.

4. Cut the excess bulk from the lining fabric at the corners, and secure it to the tape.

5. To secure the assembled piece to the inside of the lid of the suitcase, use another round of carpet tape as well as hot glue or heavy-duty glue.

6. For the base of the suitcase, attach ribbons to the base lining piece as desired before attaching it to the foam core. The ribbons can be use to hold plates and glasses for a picnic.

7. Follow the instructions above for attaching the lid lining to the inside of the suitcase lid to attach the base lining to the inside of the suitcase base.

Storm at Sea

DIMENSIONS: 50" x 58½" (127 x 148.5cm)

The inspiration for this quilt came from a vintage embroidered tablecloth. Three corners boast motifs exclaiming "Storm at Sea," "Ships Ahoy," and "Anchors Aweigh." When spelled out using the Nautical Flag Alphabet, these words make a striking border. The Storm at Sea block is particularly visually graphic and a great choice for this quilt. Reproduction fabrics from the 20s, 30s, and 40s add to the nostalgia. This quilt is a sunny, happy piece that sets a festive scene for any deck party.

J. HORN

Fabric Requirements

☐ ½–¾ yd. (50–75cm) novelty print (amount varies due to the spacing of the motif)

☐ ⅔ yd. (67cm) dark blue

☐ 3–4 fat quarters (45.5 x 56cm) assorted dark blue prints

☐ I yd. (100cm) blue and white stripe (includes bias binding)

☐ ¾ yd. (75cm) yellow

☐ I yd. (100cm) red

☐ I–2 fat quarters (45.5 x 56cm) assorted red prints

☐ I yd. (100cm) white with blue background

☐ ⅓ yd. (33cm) white with red background

☐ I fat quarter (45.5 x 56cm) white

☐ Backing and batting

The motifs on these linens inspired the Nautical Flag borders on this quilt.

N block

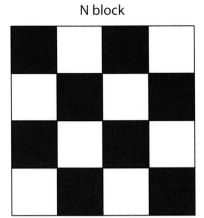

Make 1 block

1. Cut four 1½" x 3" (4 x 7.5cm) strips from the dark blue.

2. Cut four 1½" x 3" (4 x 7.5cm) strips from the white.

3. Sew 4 of the strips together along the long edges, alternating each color. Then, cut them into 1½" (4cm) pieced units: dark blue, white, dark blue, white.

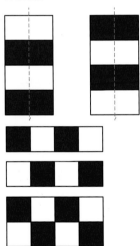

4. Sew the remaining strips, alternating white, dark blue, white, dark blue. Then, cut them the same as you did in Step 3.

5. Sew the strips together, making sure the seams are pressed in opposing directions for a great fit. Trim the block to 4½" (11.5cm).

O block

Make 3 blocks

1. Cut one 4⅞" x 4⅞" (12.5 x 12.5cm) square from the yellow, and crosscut it diagonally once.

2. Cut one 4⅞" x 4⅞" (12.5 x 12.5cm) square from the red, and crosscut it diagonally once. You will need 1 half-square triangle in each color for each block; save the remaining triangles for future blocks.

3. Sew the pieces together as shown. Make 3 blocks, and trim them to 4½" (11.5cm).

P block

Make 1 block

1. Cut one 2½" x 2½" (6.5cm) square from the white fabric.

2. Cut two 1½" x 2½" (4 x 6.5cm) rectangles from the dark blue fabric

3. Cut two 1½" x 4½" (4 x 11.5cm) rectangles from the dark blue fabric.

4. Sew the pieces together as shown. Make 1 block, and trim it to 4½" (11.5cm).

R BLOCK

R block

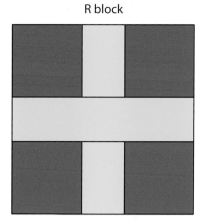

Make 2 blocks

1. Cut four 2" x 2" (5 x 5cm) squares from the red.

2. Cut two 1½" x 2" (4 x 5cm) rectangles from the yellow.

3. Cut one 1½" x 4½" (4 x 11.5cm) rectangle from yellow.

4. Sew the pieces together as shown. Make 2 blocks, and trim them to 4½" (11.5cm).

T BLOCK

T block

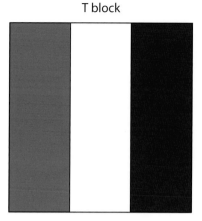

Make 2 blocks

1. Cut one 1¾" x 4½" (4.5 x 11.5cm) rectangle from the red.

2. Cut one 2" x 4½" (5 x 11.5cm) rectangle from the white.

3. Cut one 1¾" x 4½" (4.5 x 11.5cm) rectangle from the dark blue.

4. Sew the pieces together as shown. Make 2 blocks, and trim them to 4½" (11.5cm).

S BLOCK

S block

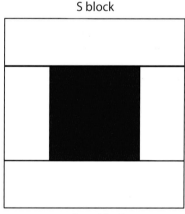

Make 5 blocks

Use the same method for the P block to make 5 S blocks, but use dark blue fabric for the center square and white fabric for the rectangles. Make 5 blocks and trim them to 4½" (11.5cm).

W BLOCK

W block

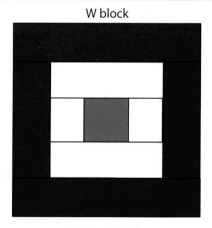

Make 1 block

1. Cut one 1½" x 1½" (4 x 4cm) square from the red.

2. Cut two 1¼" x 1½" (3 x 4cm) rectangles and two 1¼" x 3" (3 x 7.5cm) rectangles from the white.

3. Cut two 1¼" x 3" (3 x 7.5cm) rectangles and two 1¼" x 4½" (3 x 11.5cm) rectangles from the dark blue.

4. Sew the pieces together as shown. Make 1 block, and trim it to 4½" (11.5cm).

Y block

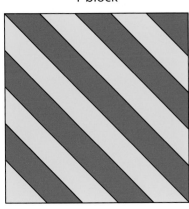

Make 1 block

1. Cut five 1" x 6½" (2.5 x 16.5cm) strips from both the red and the yellow fabrics.

2. Sew the strips together along the long edges, alternating each color.

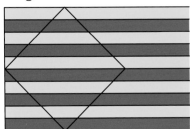

3. Cut out a 4½" x 4½" (11.5 x 11.5cm) square from the sheet of strips on a 45° angle and trim it to 4½" (11.5cm).

1. Cut one 2" x 2" (5 x 5cm) square from the dark blue.

2. Cut one 3½" x 3½" (9 x 9cm) square from the white, and then crosscut it diagonally twice from corner to corner. You will need 2 of the resulting quarter-square triangles for each block.

3. Cut two 2⅛" x 8" (5.5 x 20.5cm) strips from the white.

4. Cut one 6¼" x 6¼" (16 x 16cm) square from the white, and then crosscut it diagonally once.

5. Cut one 2" x 4¾" (5 x 12cm) rectangle from the red.

6. Cut one 1½" x 8" (4 x 20.5cm) strip and two 1½" x 5" (4 x 12.5cm) strips from the red.

7. Assemble all the pieces for the Anchor block except for the 1½" x 5" (4 x 12.5cm) red strips. Trim the block to 8½" (21.5cm)

Trim to 8½" (21.5cm)

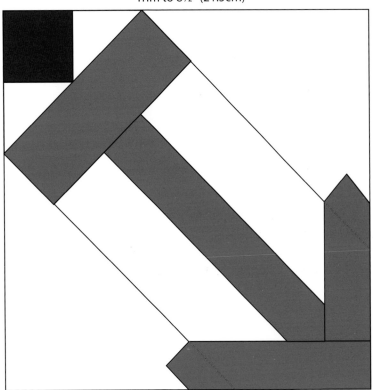

Make 2 blocks

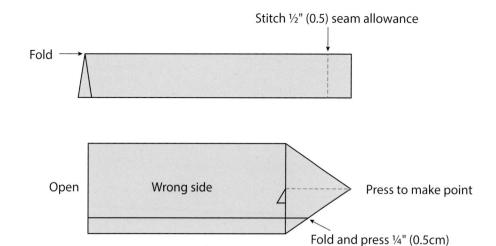

Stitch ½" (0.5) seam allowance

Fold →

Open   Wrong side   Press to make point

Fold and press ¼" (0.5cm)
seam allowance

8. Fold the 1½" x 5" (4 x 12.5cm) red strips in half lengthwise with right sides together, and stitch a seam down one short end. Open the fold, and press the tip into a point. Press under ¼" (0.5cm) on one long side of each red strip. Place the strips on the corner of the block to create the point of the anchor. Appliqué the strips in place using an edge stitch or by hand. Make 2 blocks.

PIECED BORDER ASSEMBLY

Add the borders to the quilt. Note: Each nautical flag block is separated by a 1½" x 4½" (4 x 11.5cm) spacing strip. The filler units at the beginning and end of each border may vary, as these are called coping strips. The goal is to have the border match the quilt top measurements.

FINISHING

1. Mark the quilt top using a design of your choice.

2. Layer the quilt top with the batting and backing; baste it in place.

3. Quilt as desired, and then bind the edges.

4. Add a label, and sign, date, and photograph your finished quilt.

Seaside Style:
Nautical Pillows

Each pillow is made from a traditional quilt block that can be related to the beach theme:
- 12½" (32cm) Summer Winds block on point (makes an 18" [45.5cm] pillow)
- 12½" (32cm) Nautilus block
- 16" (41cm) Milky Way block
- 9" (23cm) Waves of the Sea block on point (makes a 16" [41cm] pillow)

Supplies

- ☐ Scraps or fabric to form the front pillow block
- ☐ Pillow backing fabric
- ☐ Binding
- ☐ Muslin
- ☐ Pillow form
- ☐ Batting
- ☐ Zipper
- ☐ Buttons (optional)

Project Directions

1. Layer the block, batting, and muslin (this will be on the inside of the pillow), and baste them together. Quilt the pillow front.

2. From the backing fabric, cut 1 piece the same size as the entire pillow and 1 piece 1½ times the size of the entire pillow. Example: If your pillow measures 12" x 12" (30.5 x 30.5cm), cut one 12" x 12" (30.5 x 30.5cm) piece and one 12" x 18" (30.5 x 45.5cm). Note: Because the pillow backing is made of two pieces of fabric that are doubled over and will overlap, it does not need to be lined. The overlap conceals the zipper and could have buttons for a fun touch and an optional look.

3. Fold each of the fabric backing pieces in half so they now measure 6" x 12" (15 x 30.5cm) and 9" x 12" (23 x 30.5cm).

4. Sew one half of the zipper to the folded edge of the 6" x 12" (15 x 30.5cm) piece.

5. Lay the 2 backing pieces on the back side of the pillow top with right sides together. Place the larger piece first, and then the smaller piece with the sewn zipper. Adjust the backing pieces as necessary so they align with the pillow top. Note: This gives a visual reference as to where to place the other zipper half on the large backing piece. Mark the zipper placement.

6. Topstitch from the zipper side along the edge of the zipper to attach it to the large backing piece.

7. With wrong sides together, attach the pillow front and back by stitching around the outside edges.

8. Bind the edges. Then, insert the pillow form and enjoy!

Nautilus

Milky Way

Summer Winds

Waves of the Sea

Sweet Dreams under Starry Skies Crib Quilt

DIMENSIONS: 36½" x 60½" (92.5 x 153.5cm)

Sweet dreams will surely spring to life under the warmth of this quilt. Wrap up your little one and get cozy in a rocker by the fireplace, on the porch, or in the nursery…it's time to tell stories and create memories.

The beauty of this quilt is the unexpected fracturing of the upper section. A Summer Winds block placed on point represents the moon. The twirling effect that surrounds this block, created by using pinwheels and yellow and peach colors, gives a sense of twinkling stars. Parts of the Milky Way block peek through at the corners of this section. The middle of the quilt contains Port and Starboard blocks to settle the mood, and the quilt ends with Nautilus blocks along the bottom. The entire quilt makes you wonder if Wynken, Blynken, and Nod are there somewhere under the starry skies.

J. HORN

Fabric Requirements

This quilt is all about color values. Using the values of dark, medium, medium-light, and light sets the mood and movement of the design. The darks and mediums of the purple, green, and blue of the sky set against the light yellows and peaches make the eye focus on the moon and stars. The use of medium-light to medium with a smattering of dark and a dash of light give the Port and Starboard area a more calming sea, while the darks, mediums, medium-lights, and lights promote the movement and foaming of the waves.

As you select your fabrics, consider using some batiks and hand-dyes, as these often have good transitions between colors, such as from yellow to peach and blue to green.

- [ ] From the color palette of purple, blue, and green, select values as follows:

    11 fat quarters (45.5 x 56cm) darks

    13 fat quarters (45.5 x 56cm) mediums and medium-lights

    3 fat quarters (45.5 x 56cm) lights

- [ ] From the color palette of yellow and peach, select values as follows:

    3 fat quarters (45.5 x 56cm) light to bright yellows

    1 fat quarter (45.5 x 56cm) light to medium yellow/peach batik

    4 fat quarters (45.5 x 56cm) light peach

    1 fat quarter (45.5 x 56cm) dark peach/green batik

- [ ] ½ yd. (50cm) striped fabric for binding

- [ ] Batting and backing

The splashes of yellow and peach in this quilt give the impression of twinkling stars or the sky at sunset.

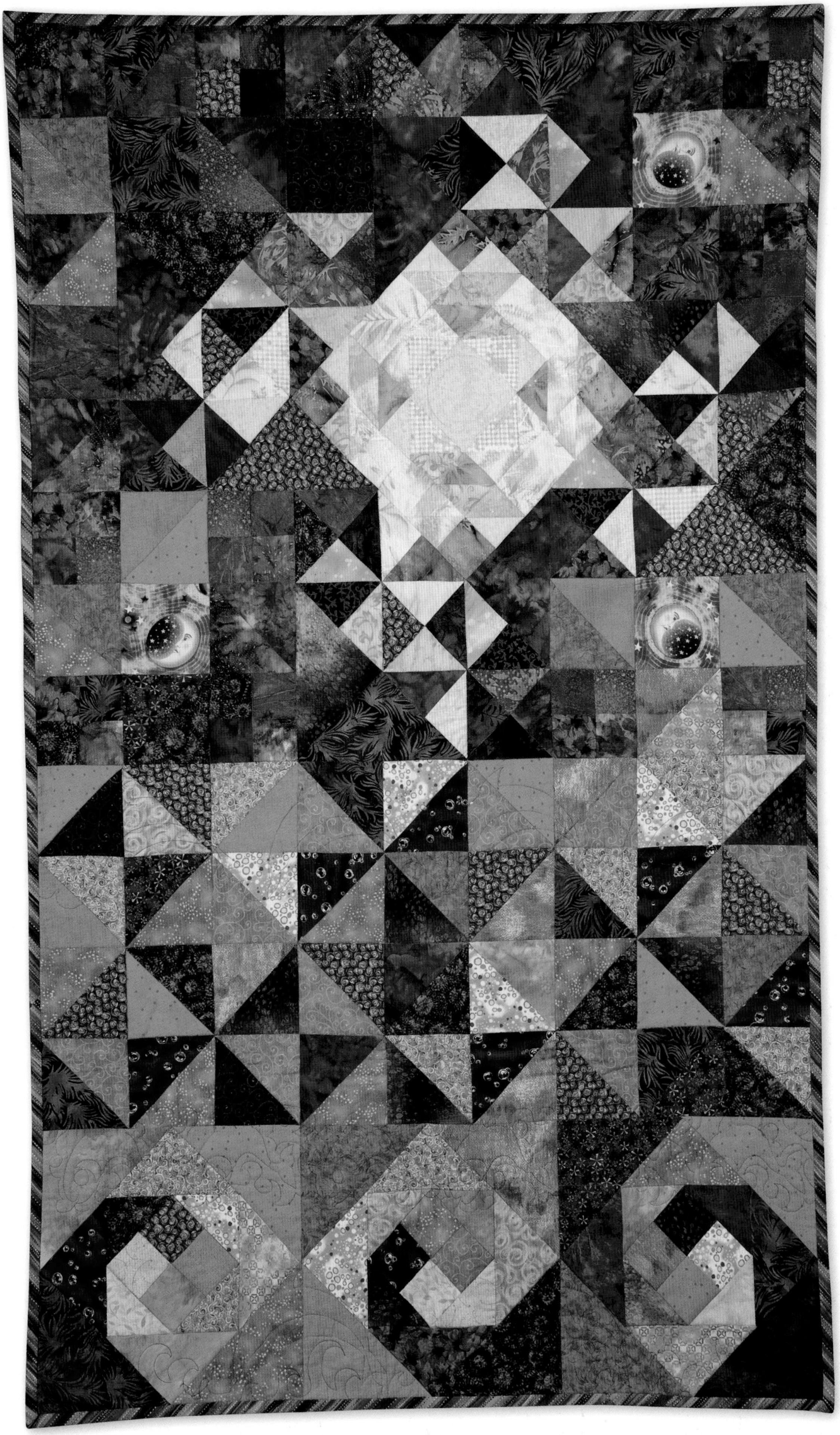

Cutting & Sewing Directions

SUMMER WINDS BLOCK

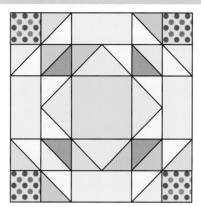

1. Cut four 2½" x 2½" (6.5 x 6.5cm) squares from the blue-green batik for the corners.

2. Cut four 2½" x 4½" (6.5 x 11.5cm) rectangles from yellow.

3. Cut one 4" x 4" (10 x 10cm) square from yellow for the center.

4. Cut four 2½" x 4" (6.5 x 10cm) rectangles and eight 2½" x 2½" (6.5 x 6.5cm) squares from yellows and peaches. Make 4 Flying Geese units (see page 29).

5. Cut six 2⅞" x 2⅞" (7.5 x ⅞cm) squares from yellows and six 2⅞" x 2⅞" (7.5 x 7.5cm) squares from peaches. Make 12 Half-Square Triangle units (see page 29).

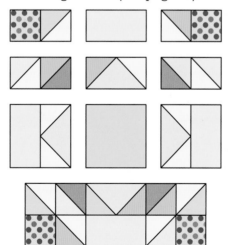

6. Lay out the block and stitch the pieces into rows. Then, stitch the rows together as illustrated. Trim the block to 12" x 12" (30.5 x 30.5cm). The finished size will be 11½" (29cm). Make 1 block.

NAUTILUS BLOCK

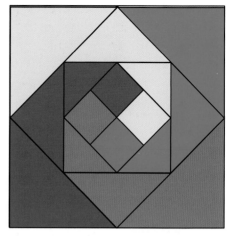

1. From the purple, blue, and green palette, cut 3 light, 3 medium-light, 3 medium, and 3 dark squares, each 2⅝" x 2⅝" (6.5 x 6.5cm). Use 1 square from each value to make 3 four-patch units (see page 115). Trim the units to 4¼" (11cm).

2. Cut two 3⅞" x 3⅞" (10 x 10cm) squares from each of the 4 values (for a total of 8 squares), and then crosscut them diagonally once. Sew 1 triangle of each value to the four-patch from Step 1. Trim the unit to 6½" (16.5cm).

3. Cut two 4⅞" x 4⅞" (12.5 x 12.5cm) squares from each of the 4 values (for a total of 8 squares), and then crosscut them diagonally once. Sew 1 triangle of each value to the unit made in Step 2. Trim the unit to 9" (23cm).

4. Cut two 6⅞" x 6⅞" (17.5 x 17.5cm) squares from each of the 4 values (for a total of 8 squares), and then crosscut them diagonally once. Sew 1 triangle of each value to the unit made in Step 3. Trim the unit to 12½" (32cm). The finished size of the unit will be 12" (30.5cm). Make 3 blocks.

5. Sew the 3 Nautilus blocks into a row.

PORT & STARBOARD BLOCKS

Make 2 blocks   Make 1 strip

1. From the purple, blue, and green palette, choose 8 assorted fabrics from the medium/medium-light fabric values and cut 18 squares, each 4⅞" x 4⅞" (12.5 x 12.5cm). Crosscut these squares diagonally once, and divide them by color into medium and medium-light stacks.

2. From the same palette, choose 8 assorted fabrics from the dark fabric values and cut 15 squares, each 4⅞" x 4⅞" (12.5 x 12.5cm). Crosscut these squares diagonally once, and place them in a stack.

3. From the same palette, choose 2 assorted fabrics from the light fabric values and cut 3 squares, each 4⅞" x 4⅞" (12.5 x 12.5cm). Crosscut these squares diagonally once, and place them in a stack.

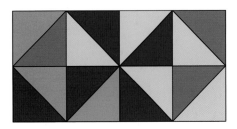

4. From the stacks, make 36 Half-Square Triangle units. Arrange and sew the units as illustrated into 2 blocks and 1 filler strip. Trim blocks to 16½" (42cm). The finished size of the blocks will be 16" (40.5cm).

5. Sew the two blocks and filler strip into a row.

TOP SECTION

The best way to approach the design work for this section is to place the Summer Winds block on point on a design wall.

Cut and sew the following units, place them around the Summer Winds block, and then sew the units together in sections as shown on page 117.

FOUR-PATCH

1. Cut forty 2½" x 2½" (6.5 x 6.5cm) squares.

2. Make 10 Four-Patch units. Trim them to 4½" (11.5cm).

HALF-SQUARE TRIANGLE UNIT

1. Cut seventeen 4⅞" x 4⅞" (12.5 x 12.5cm) squares, and then crosscut them diagonally once.

2. Make 15 Half-Square Triangle units (see page 29; leave 4 triangles unsewn). Trim them to 4½" (11.5cm).

PINWHEEL UNITS

1. Cut 5 assorted yellow, 11 assorted peach, and 23 assorted green/purple/blue squares, each 3⅞" x 3⅞" (10 x 10cm). Crosscut the squares diagonally once. Make 27 Half-Square Triangle units and trim them to 3½" (9cm).

2. From the Half-Square Triangle units, make 6 Pinwheels (you will use 4 Half-Square Triangle units for each Pinwheel). Trim them to 6½" (16.5cm).

3. Make 2 Half-Pinwheel units.

4. Make 8 Quarter-Pinwheel units.

SQUARES

1. Cut six 4½" x 4½" (11.5 x 11.5cm) squares.

LARGE HALF-SQUARE TRIANGLES

1. Cut six 6½" (16.5cm) squares. Then, crosscut the squares diagonally once.

ASSEMBLY AND FINISHING

1. With the units for the top section cut and sewn, they are now ready to go up on the design wall. Sew the sections together to make large units, and then sew the units together.

2. To complete this quilt, add the Port & Starboard row to the top section. Then, add the Nautilus row to the bottom.

3. Mark the quilt top using a design of your choice.

4. Layer the quilt top with the batting and backing; baste it in place.

5. Quilt as desired, and then bind the edges.

6. Add a label, and sign, date, and photograph your finished quilt.

Summer Winds
block on point

Seaside Style:
Bassinet Dust Ruffle

Fabric Requirements*

*Note: The following list is based on the measurements for our bassinet. See Calculating the Fabric below to learn how to measure and calculate the fabric requirements for your bassinet.

- ☐ 3½ yd. (350cm) striped fabric
- ☐ ⅓ yd. (33cm) accent fabric
- ☐ ¾ yd. (75cm) novelty print for ruffle facing
- ☐ ¾ yd. (75cm) print for hem
- ☐ 2⅜ yd. (237.5cm) of 1"–2" (2.5–5cm)-wide non-roll elastic for circumference of the bassinet

Calculating the Fabric

Measure the circumference of the bassinet, and then multiply the result by 3 for a fully gathered dust ruffle. Example: 86" (218.5cm) circumference x 3 = 258" (655.5cm).

The measurement of "usable" fabric from selvage to selvage (also known as the width of the fabric) is based on an average of 40" (104cm). There is often more than this; however, after the selvage is removed, 40" (104cm) is what you can count on for calculations. Divide your answer above by 40" (104cm) to determine the number of strips you will need. Example: 258" (655.5cm) divided by 40" (104cm) = 6.45 strips. Round this figure up and you will need to cut 7 strips.

The next measurement is the height from the top of the bassinet to the floor (or any length in between). Dust ruffles normally go to the floor to keep the "dust bunnies" from gathering under the bassinet! We added an accent strip and coordinating color at the bottom of the ruffle at a width of 2" (5cm). We subtracted this amount from the total height of the bassinet, giving us a

total height measurement of 17" (43cm). Example: 19" (48.5cm) total height – 2" (5cm) accent strip = 17" (43cm).

To calculate the amount of fabric you'll need, multiply the number of strips calculated by the height measurement calculated. Then, divide the total by 36" (or 1 yd.). For metric calculations, divide the total by 100cm (or 1m). Example: 7 strips x 17" (43cm) height = 119" (302cm). 119" (302cm) / 36" (91.5cm) = 3.30 yd. Round this figure up and you will need 3½ yd. (350cm) of fabric.

Project Directions

CUTTING

1. Cut seven 17" (43cm)-wide strips, selvage to selvage, from striped fabric.

2. Cut seven 4" (10cm)-wide strips, selvage to selvage, from the novelty print.

3. Cut seven 4" (10cm)-wide strips, selvage to selvage, from the hem print.

4. Cut seven 1½" (4cm)-wide strips, selvage to selvage, from the accent print.

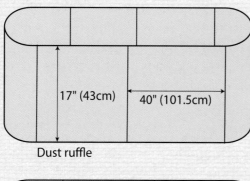

Dust ruffle

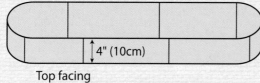

Top facing

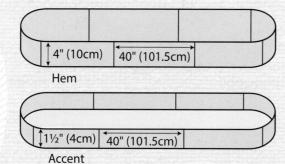

Hem

Accent

CONSTRUCTION

1. All of the sections for the dust ruffle need to be the same length. Because manufacturers do not always produce fabric in the same width, you will need to measure and trim your strips to the same measurement before sewing them together. Fold the cut strips in half lengthwise and layer them on top of each other to determine which strip is the shortest. Then, cut all the strips to this length.

2. Sew the striped strips together along the short edges using straight seams (or a French seam).

3. Sew the short ends of all the strips together to form tubes.

UPPER RUFFLE FACING AND ELASTIC CASING

1. Sew the novelty print to the top edge of the striped fabric with right sides together. If the print has a direction, place it upside down so it will be right side up when it is pressed to the back. This is the facing for the top ruffle and the casing for the elastic. Press the ¼" (0.5cm) seam allowance to the facing.

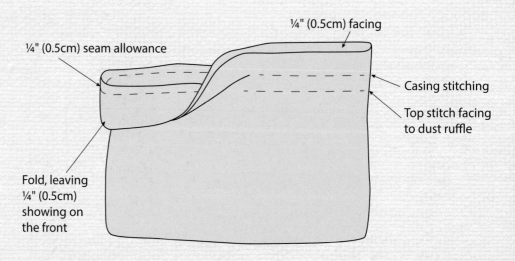

2. Press under ¼" (0.5cm) of the raw edge of the facing. Then, press the facing toward the wrong side of the dust ruffle with ¼" (0.5cm) of the facing showing on the right side. Edge stitch the facing to the dust ruffle.

3. For the casing, add ¼" (0.5cm) to the width of the elastic. Example: 1¼" (4cm)-wide elastic should have a 1¾" (4.5cm)-wide casing. Using this measurement, measure up from the seam attaching the facing to the dust ruffle. Sew from this point around the entire dust ruffle to form the top of the casing.

HEM EDGE

1. With wrong sides together, press the 1½" (4cm) accent strip in half lengthwise.

2. Stitch the accent strip to the hem strip with right sides together. Press seam to the hem.

3. Pin the unsewn edge of the hem strip, wrong side facing out, to the wrong side of the dust ruffle, and stitch it in place. Press the seam allowance to the hem strip. Fold the hem strip in half, and bring it to the front. Top stitch the hem in place at the seam line of the accent piece.

FINISHING

Open up 1 seam to the casing on the facing side using a seam ripper so that you can insert the elastic. Use a large safety pin attached to the elastic to pull it through the casing. Pull up on the ends of the elastic to gather the fabric. Adjust the elastic to the proper fit for the bassinet, and then sew the ends together. The elastic will pop back into the casing and you can hand sew the opening closed.

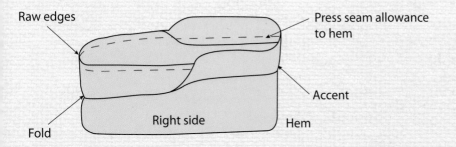

Raw edges · Press seam allowance to hem · Accent · Fold · Right side · Hem

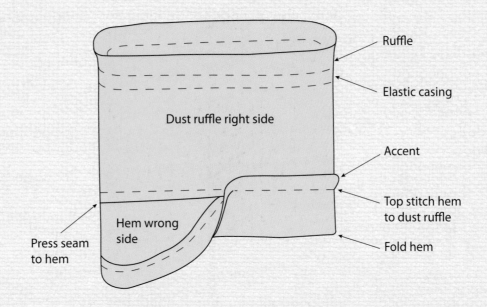

Ruffle · Elastic casing · Dust ruffle right side · Accent · Top stitch hem to dust ruffle · Fold hem · Press seam to hem · Hem wrong side

Techniques

These three quilting techniques can be used to finish or add appliqué to any of the quilt projects in this book, or any future project you might wish to make.

Gathered bed skirts can add a calming touch to an adult's room.

Gently gathered stripe bed skirts are very generic. They work well for a boy's room.

Bed Skirt Basics

Bed skirts can be simple or complex and are a wonderful way to bring a special touch to the finished look of any bedroom. Highly gathered ruffles, modified gathers, either side of a box pleat, and multiple layers are some of the many options. Reversible bed skirts with a spring/ summer fabric on one side and fall/winter on the other offer a simple change in mood and color for the room. We suggest prewashing all of the fabrics used in the bed skirts.

Base

All bed skirts need a base to go between the mattress and box spring. Because this portion of the bed skirt does not show, a used, but not worn, bed sheet is ideal for the base. Another option is quilt backing fabric, as it is wide enough that it won't require any seams.

Measure the top of the mattress and add 1" (2.5cm) on all sides. Cut the fabric for the base of the bed skirt using a rotary cutter and mat to ensure all the edges are straight and even.

Bed Styles

A footboard or poster bed needs a three-section skirt with hems on the edges by the corners. All other beds use a continuous horizontal piece that goes around three sides.

Each style uses a 6" (15cm) return on the headboard end. This will not show, but fabric going around the corner gives a finished look.

Project Directions for a Continuous Gathered Bed Skirt

1. Measure vertically from the point that the bed skirt connects with the base of the bed to the length desired. This is called the "drop" of the main skirt.

2. For the base fabric, which is typically placed between the mattress and the box spring and holds the ruffle in place, measure the length of the 2 sides and end of the bed.

3. For the gathered skirt you'll need 2½–3 times more fabric than the total length measurements of the sides and end of the bed, plus 12" (30.5cm). This allows extra fabric for hemming the vertical ends at the

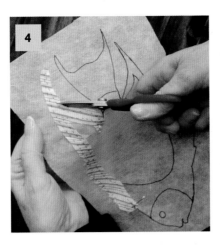

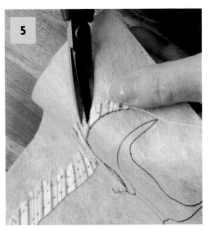

Trim. Turn the interfacing to the right side and trim a scant ¼" (0.5cm) around the outside of the basting.

Clip the seam allowances. Look at the pattern and determine the edges that will be needle turned. Mark the beginning and end of the needle turned edges. Clip up to the stitch line at these points, making diagonal clips in the seam allowance.

Clip the basting stitches. Clip the basting stitches at every ½" (1.5cm), but do not remove the stitches.

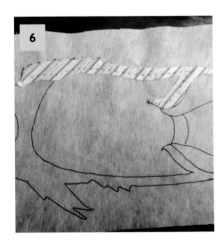

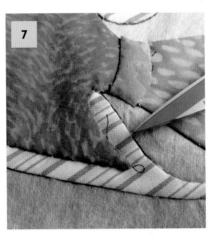

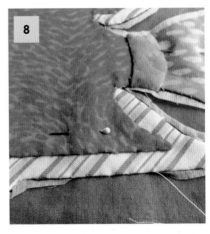

Turn under the seam allowances. Thread the appliqué needle with thread and make a knot in the end. Remove the first ½" (1.5cm) of basting thread and begin needle turning the seam allowance. Remove the basting threads as you go until you have come to the ending point. Tie the thread to the back. Do not remove the basting stitches from any part that will be overlapped. These basting stitches will become the sewing line for the piece that will go on top.

Add the remaining pieces. Stitch any remaining appliqué pieces to the interfacing. Then, remove all the basting stitches.

Sew to the quilt. Trim the interfacing to ⅛" (0.5cm) around the edges of the appliqué piece. Position the appliqué on to the quilt, and pin or baste it in place. Needle turn the interfacing well under the appliqué, clipping as necessary at curves and notches.

Raw-Edge Appliqué

This technique is fun and easy and requires no "needle turning" of the seam allowance and no hand sewing. The raw edge will fray, leaving a wonderful dimension to the appliquéd pieces. The appliqué is layered from the back forward as in traditional appliqué. Each piece is stitched down approximately ⅛"– ¼" (0.5cm) away from the cut edge.

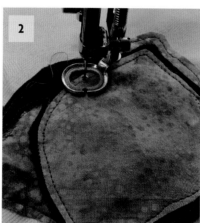

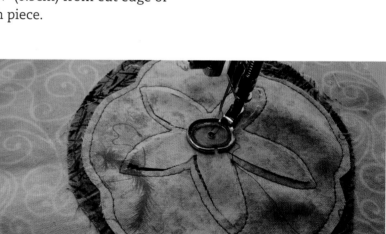

Tip

Washing will fray the edges of the appliqué. A nail brush can also be used to rough up the edges.

Prepare the fabric. For each motif, trace the pieces to be appliquéd onto the selected fabrics. No seam allowance is necessary. The designs are numbered in order of placement. This raw-edge method always starts with a piece of fabric cut from the entire outline as a base. Then, you will apply the numbered pieces.

Stitch the layers. Edge-stitch ⅛"–¼" (0.5cm) from cut edge of each piece.

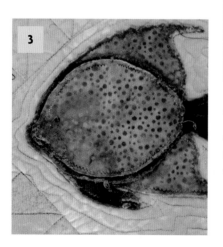

Attach to the quilt. Stitch the appliqué piece onto the quilt.

The top layer of fabric for the sand dollar has a star cut from it. After stitching the top layer of fabric in place, edge-stitch around all sides of the cut star to hold it in place. When the quilt is washed, the star will be exposed as the cut edges fray.

Appliqué and Embroidery Patterns

Sand Treasures Patterns (pages 36–41)

Enlarge all 200%

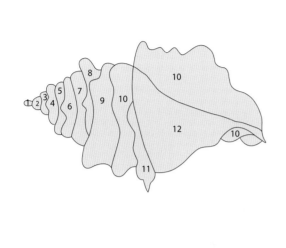

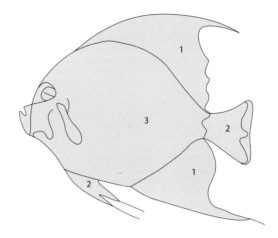

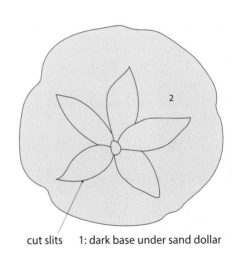

cut slits   1: dark base under sand dollar

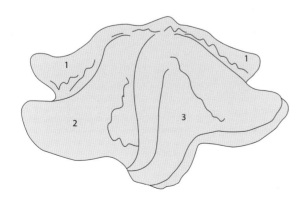

Sand Treasures Patterns (pages 36–41)

Enlarge all 200%

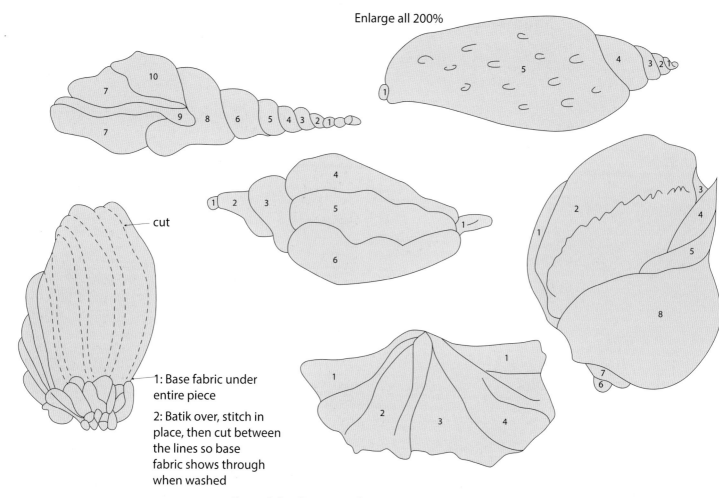

cut

1: Base fabric under entire piece

2: Batik over, stitch in place, then cut between the lines so base fabric shows through when washed

Seaside Serenade Patterns (pages 54–59)

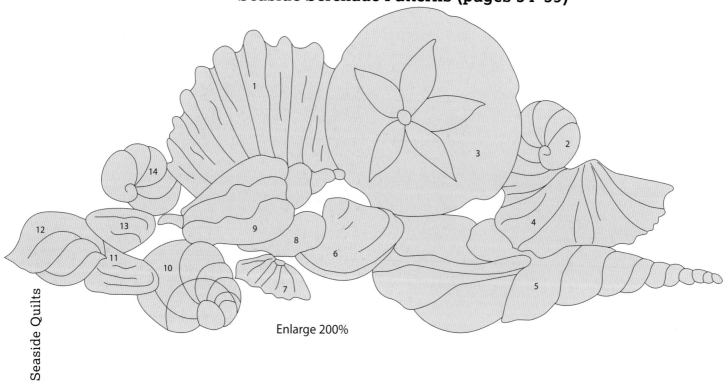

Enlarge 200%

**Seaside Serenade/
Seaside Bounty Patterns
(pages 54–61)**

Enlarge 360%

Start with the vase base (#1 and #1a).
Then, work the vase appliqué (#2 and #3).
Note: #2 for the vase appliqué can be cut
from one piece of fabric with the #3 pieces
appliquéd over top. Then, add the upper
rim of the vase (#5, #5a, and #5b).

A Day at the Beach Patterns (pages 80–89)

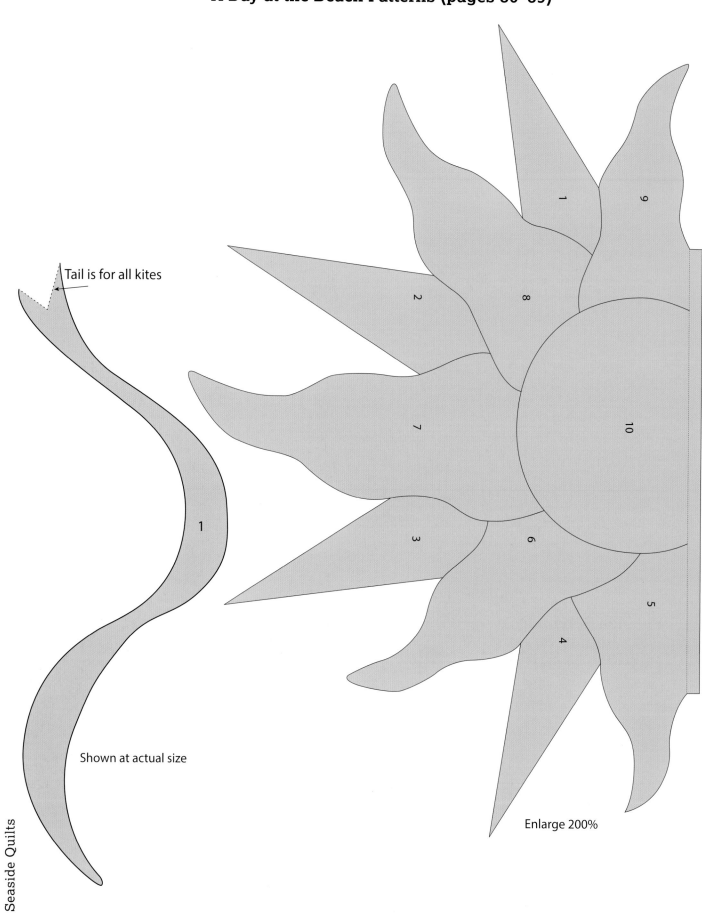

Tail is for all kites

1

2

8

1

9

7

10

3

6

5

4

Shown at actual size

Enlarge 200%

A Day at the Beach Patterns (pages 80–89)

Enlarge all 200%

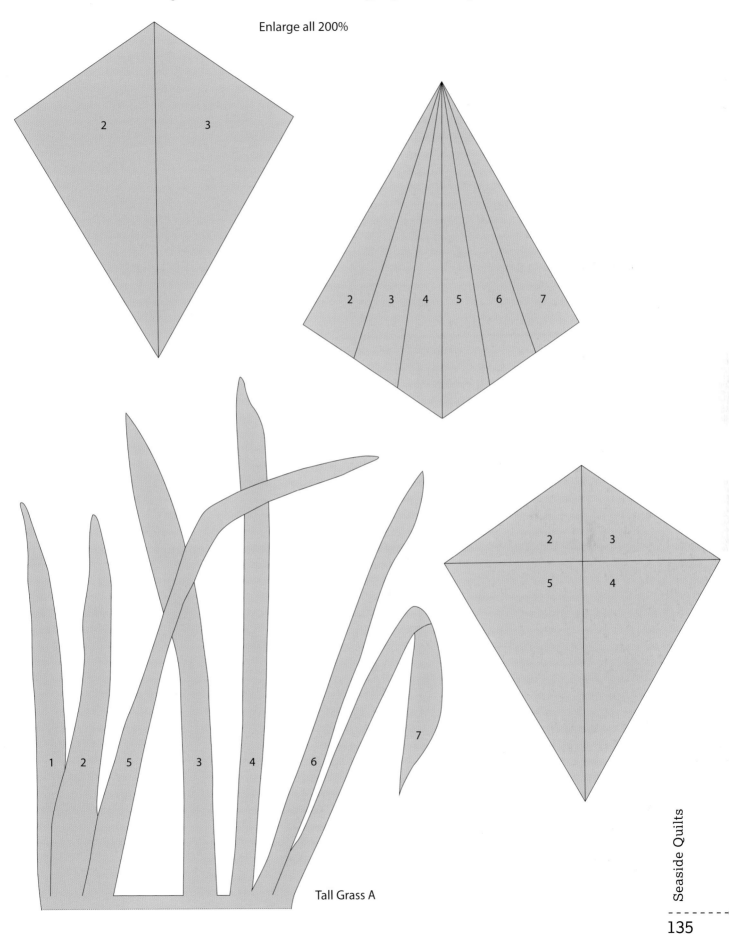

Tall Grass A

Patterns

A Day at the Beach Patterns (pages 80–89)

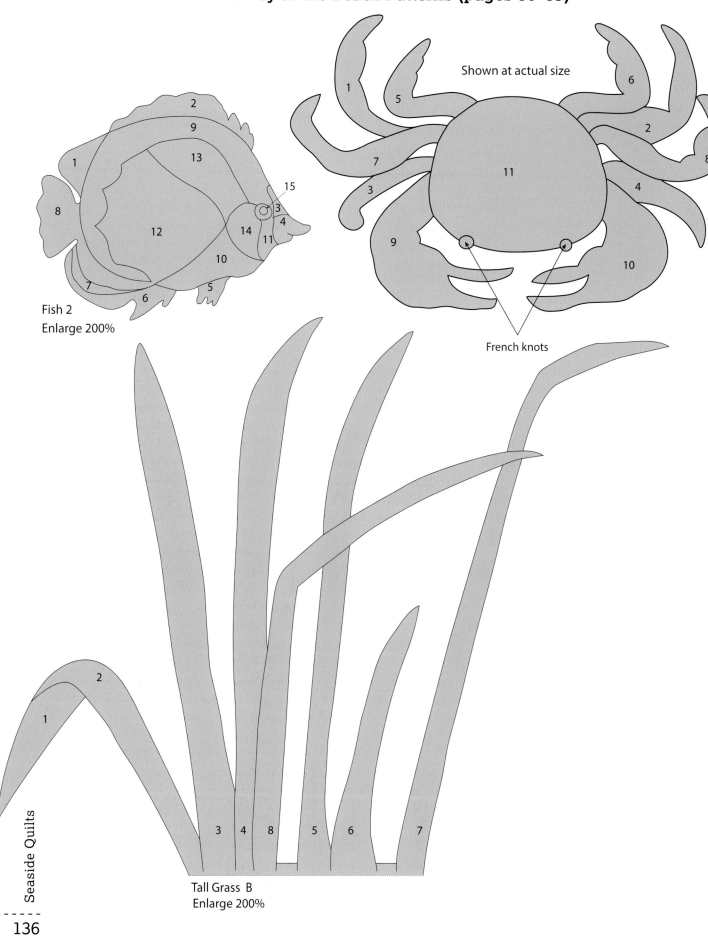

Shown at actual size

Fish 2
Enlarge 200%

French knots

Tall Grass B
Enlarge 200%

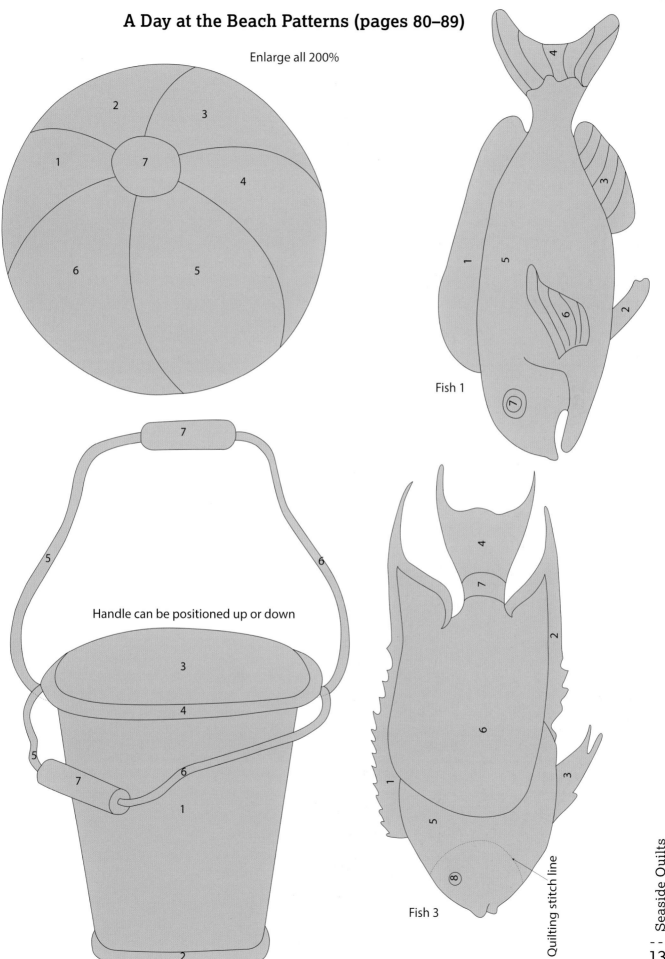

A Day at the Beach Patterns (pages 80–89)

Enlarge all 200%

Fish 1

Handle can be positioned up or down

Fish 3

Quilting stitch line

A Day at the Beach Patterns (pages 86–89)

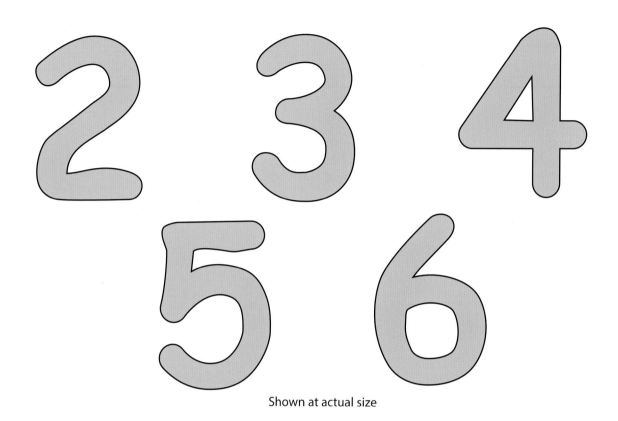

Shown at actual size

Optional Embroidery Pattern

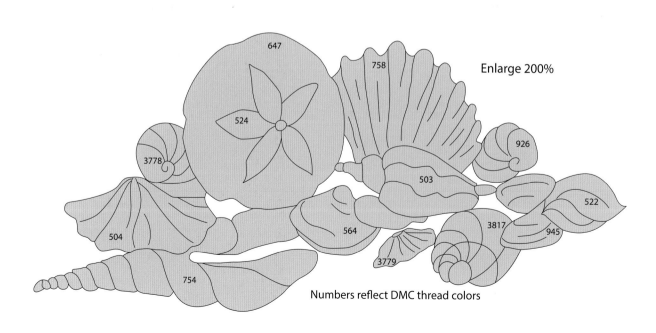

Enlarge 200%

Numbers reflect DMC thread colors

Storm at Sea Templates (pages 100–108)

Shown at actual size

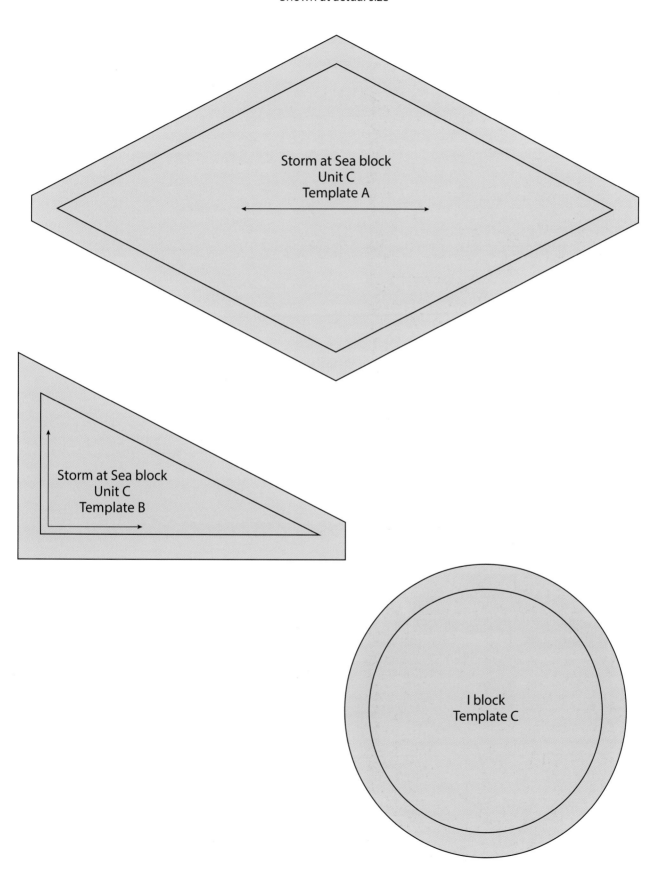

Storm at Sea block
Unit C
Template A

Storm at Sea block
Unit C
Template B

I block
Template C

Acknowledgments

Dedicated to my parents—my mom for inspiring me with her love of sewing at a very young age and my dad for his work ethic and can-do attitude. He encouraged me to challenge myself and do my best, and told me I could do anything I put my mind to. Their life lessons live on and inspire.

My heartfelt gratitude to Carol for suggesting we do this project together—your friendship, encouragement, and attention to detail are immeasurable.

Many thanks to my high school home economics teacher, Ms. Miller, who started me on this journey with a strong foundation.

To Donna McMahon, my first neighbor as a homeowner and young mother. I learned so much from you and love that you suggested we take decorative painting classes and quilting classes. Oh the seeds you planted.

Most important, thanks to my family, who support and inspire me. From pajamas to prom dress, Halloween to skating costumes, and soccer to cheer uniforms, you have been there for it all. When your sports were finished, the quilting journey began. To my husband, Bruce, who is always ready to scout out antique and quilt shops. Your help with construction, furnishings, photo shoots, and patience during this journey has been a blessing.

To the great Northwest for its beauty and the diversity of its landscape. I have unending inspiration everywhere I look and an abundance of teachers, authors, guilds, and quilt shops to fuel and feed my passion.

To the Laid Back Ladies of the Block for their inspiration, friendship, and support. To Betty Howland for helping with the wired rocks and the last photo shoot.

To Donna Ferrill, who without hesitation did our embroidery work. You are always there for support, a road trip, or just as a sounding board. You are my sister by choice and thankfully just a phone call away.

To Fox Chapel for believing in us and our vision for this book.

—Beckie

Many, many thanks to:

Judith McCabe and Peg Couch for believing in our vision that quilts and projects with a beach and cottage theme have universal appeal.

Beckie Hansen, whose creative mind and fast fingers give beauty to her home, quilts, and all she touches. You so often think outside the box and are willing to step up and try new things. You are a true lesson in "if you can dream it, you can do it."

Katie Weeber, what an extraordinary editor! It's a pleasure to work with someone who knows exactly what you mean.

The Fox Chapel team, who consistently blow me away with their layout and artistic magic.

The Laid Back Ladies of the Block. Your emotional support for Beckie and me means the world to us.

My husband, David. You always have the right words at the right time and the right place. What a blessing you are to me. I am grateful to have you and our family by my side.

–Carol

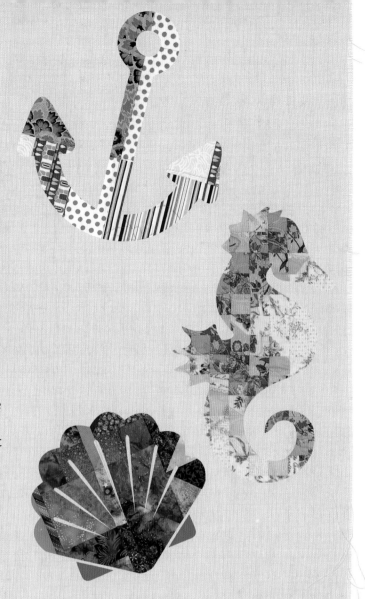

Resources:

We would like to thank the following for providing the materials and tools we needed to make these wonderful projects:

Dolores' Antiques & Collectibles, Ocean Shores, Washington, for its abundant collection of vintage linens and many basket linen finds.

Clover Needlecraft Incorporated for many quality tools that gave us fabulous results.

The Warm Company for Lite Steam-A-Seam 2.

The sea and shores for what you gave us in treasures and inspiration.

Index

Note: Page numbers in *italics* indicate projects/patterns.

More Great Books from Design Originals

**All My Thanks and
Love to Quilts**
ISBN 978-1-57421-425-3 **$24.99**
DO5396

Five-Minute Quilt Blocks
ISBN 978-1-57421-420-8 **$18.99**
DO5391

Sewing Pretty Little Things
ISBN 978-1-57421-611-0 **$19.99**
DO5301

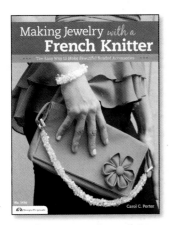

**Making Jewelry with
a French Knitter**
ISBN 978-1-57421-363-8 **$8.99**
DO3486

Crazy Quilt Christmas Stockings
ISBN 978-1-57421-360-7 **$8.99**
DO3483

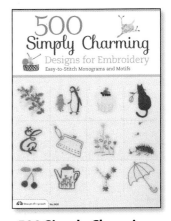

**500 Simply Charming
Designs for Embroidery**
ISBN 978-1-57421-509-0 **$14.99**
DO5430

Quilting & Applique
ISBN 978-1-57421-502-1 **$9.99**
DO5423

**Quilted Projects with
Wool and Wool Felt**
ISBN 978-1-57421-727-8 **$17.99**
DO5047

Designer Cross Stitch Projects
ISBN 978-1-57421-721-6 **$16.99**
DO5041

Look for These Books at Your Local Bookstore or Specialty Retailer or at *www.D-Originals.com*